The Summer of Cecily

The Summer of Cecily
by Nan Lincoln

with illustrations by
Sam White

BUNKER HILL PUBLISHING
BOSTON

First published in 2004
by Bunker Hill Publishing Inc.
26 Adams Street,
Charlestown, MA 02129 USA

10 9 8 7 6 5 4 3 2 1

Library of Congress Cataloguing in Publication Data
is available from the publisher's office

ISBN 1 59373 034 9

Designed by Louise Millar

Printed in the USA by Henry N Sawyer Company, Inc.

For Benjamin and Alexandra Lincoln, the wonderful
children I got to keep; my brilliant and beautiful
daughter-in-law, Krista Conley Lincoln; my handsome
grandchildren, James and Nicholas Lincoln,
(and any others who may come along); and finally to
my adventurous mom, Midge Stafford, who was trekking
in the Himalayas while I was swimming with seals.

Photo Credits

Acknowledgements

If it hadn't been for some gentle — well, not so gentle really —
nudging from my publishers, Ib Bellew and Carole Kitchel at
Bunker Hill, I'd still be thinking about writing this book
someday. I thank them for that and for their enthusiasm,
encouragement, guidance, and good humor throughout this
interesting process. Thanks also to my friend and fellow seal
mom Ellen Dupuy for letting me borrow her stories and take
back my own; to my friend and neighbor Nicols Fox, whose
suggestions were always right on the mark; to Steve Katona
for letting me be Cecily's mom for that extraordinary
summer; to my cousin Nan Eliot Ulett for some very necessary Scrabble breaks; and to my editor at the *Bar Harbor Times*,
Greg Fish, and the rest of the *Times* crew for their enduring
patience while I moonlighted on this book.

Foreword

It is January, always a very cold month in eastern Maine, but especially cold as this book goes to press in 2004. Ice covers the upper portions of the bays where harbor seal mothers will give birth to their pups five months from now. A few harbor seals brave the cold waters, but most have migrated south to spend winter around Cape Cod or farther south to Long Island.

Twenty-eight years have passed since the summer that Nan Lincoln and her family adopted Cecily and served as her foster parents. Nan is now a writer and Arts Editor for the *Bar Harbor Times*. The special obituaries she writes to memorialize notable citizens of Mt. Desert Island are, well, to die for. Cecily's foster sister and brother are young adults now. Alexandra graduated from College of the Atlantic and is an actress in New York. Ben graduated from the Boston Museum School of Fine Arts, has a wife and two children, and is building a house in Vermont.

College of the Atlantic has grown up, too. There are 260 undergraduate and masters students working toward their degrees in Human Ecology. Students, faculty, and research associates at the college's marine mammal research group, Allied Whale, still study the ecology and population biology of humpback whales, fin whales, and others, and collaborate with the northeast marine mammal stranding network to rescue dozens of seal pups each year.

Thanks to Acadia National Park and a number of very active land trusts, particularly the Maine Coast Heritage Trust, the Blue Hill Trust, and the Frenchman's Bay Conservancy, much of the coastline of Mt. Desert Island, including many offshore islands, remains open to people and wildlife, including harbor seals like Cecily.

When Cecily was a pup in 1976, approximately 6,000 harbor seals lived along the Maine coast. Today there are more than 25,000. In addition, other species of seals also inhabit Maine that Cecily would not have seen in her youth. Gray seals have increased in numbers from perhaps a hundred or so during her youth to several thousand now, and the population is still growing fast. Arctic species, particularly hooded seals, but also ringed seals and harp seals, are now fairly common visitors in winter, though all were quite rare here in the 1970s. All these populations have increased as a result of continued protection provided by the Marine Mammal Protection Act, initially passed by the U.S. Congress in 1972, as well as other protective legislation enacted in Canada.

Broader changes in the marine environment have also occurred since Cecily's birth. The populations of many fish species, especially cod, haddock, flounder, and dogfish sharks, for example, have decreased markedly as a result of overfishing. The population of herring, which would certainly have been one of Cicely's staple foods, also declined markedly, though it appears to have recovered in recent years. On the other hand, there are many more lobsters now, perhaps because there are fewer fishes to prey on young lobsters.

It is possible that Cecily may still come to Mt. Desert Island in summer and may actually have seen all of these changes herself. A harbor seal can live for thirty years or more in captivity when provided with good veterinary care, so a vigorous, lucky individual might also live that long in the wild.

If Cecily is still alive, she could have given birth to more than twenty pups after she became sexually mature at age three or four years. And her female pups could in time have borne their own pups. Thus Cecily could have dozens of descendants by now. The same would be true for all the other female pups born in 1976. But if that happened, Maine would be knee-deep in harbor seals and the pile would be growing fast. Since that hasn't happened, it is obvious that most harbor seals don't survive and reproduce successfully every year. If Nan had not rescued and raised her, Cecily would surely have been one of the seals who died.

Times have changed in other ways, too. Today we recommend that stranded seal pups be observed, but not disturbed, for twenty-four hours, because we know that a mother may sometimes remain apart from her pup for that long. Furthermore, foster mothers such as Nan are no longer permitted to raise abandoned pups, although permission may be granted for individuals to care for a pup overnight until transport to a veterinarian facility can be arranged. This is probably for the best, since few families are able to dedicate the time and care to raising a pup as Nan's family did.

Much more is known about the needs of seal pups than was known in 1976. For example, pups are no longer fed formulas based on cow milk or cream, because seals cannot digest lactose, the most abundant sugar in bovine milk. Newborn pups are now fed a mixture of amino acids combined with liquid B-vitamin complex. Later in their first week, their formula is a mixture of ground herring, water, milk matrix, plus the lactose-digesting enzyme, lactase, multivitamins enhanced with B-complex and vitamin B1, and table salt.

There also is a better inventory of diseases which affect pups and methods for treating some of them. Concern that some diseases can be transmitted to humans is another reason why abandoned seal pups are not placed in private homes.

So Cecily was a very lucky seal, but anyone who reads her story is lucky, too. It is our good fortune that Nan Lincoln not only raised Cecily so successfully, but tells the story so well. Nan's recounting of her family's days with Cecily is not only an engaging portrait of human and animal behavior, but also a delightful remembrance of bygone days on our island and in its communities.

Now, more than a quarter century later, the pace of life here has quickened, particularly in summer. There are more boats, kayakers, whale watchers, and tourists of every sort, and the number of summer homes has also increased. Victor and Ruby Higgins died some years ago and the A.V. Higgins general store, where Nan bought Cicely's baby bottle, formula ingredients, and food, now sells antiques. Nevertheless, the flavor and charm of the island remains much as Nan described it.

Visitors to Mt. Desert Island in summer can easily view harbor seals as well as gray seals. Seals are frequently seen swimming not far from shore, and observers equipped with binoculars or a telescope may also watch seals basking at low tide on a number of the half-tide ledges surrounding the island. Those wanting a closer look can embark on one of the tour boats operating out of the island's major towns, Bar Harbor, Northeast Harbor or Southwest Harbor, since many cruises feature a visit to a seal colony. And who knows but that you might see Cecily there, or at least one of her great, great, great grandchildren.

— Steven Katona
January 26, 2004

Abandoned Seal Adopts Pretty Marsh Family

"Cecily, the baby seal, has adopted a family in Pretty Marsh to replace the loss of her own.

Her finder contacted the proper authorities and was advised to leave the seal undisturbed to see if the mother would return. After eight hours, it was fairly obvious that the baby seal had been abandoned.

Cecily should not be mistaken for a pet. Seals are wild animals. It is illegal in the State of Maine to make a pet of a seal. Should you find a youngster apparently abandoned on the shore you should notify the proper authorities. This family is devoting a lot of time and money to see that this seal winds up healthy and thriving in her natural habitat." — Bar Harbor Times, *June 10, 1976*

Actually I only waited six hours before taking Cecily home, but it felt like six days. And no, she should never be mistaken for a pet. But for one amazing summer, she allowed me to be her mother.

— Nan Lincoln, November 2, 2003

Chapter One

The day Cecily came into our lives was miserable.

It didn't so much dawn as reluctantly materialize through a thick gray ceiling of overcast and drizzling fog. Pretty typical of early May in Maine, actually, where spring is rarely the glorious rebirth of nature's wonders it's hyped up to be in poetry and song — sunshine, wildflowers and all that nice stuff — but rather a big, sucking mess of mud, mist and bone-chilling cold. In fact, around here spring is often called mud season, or else it's called blackfly season. Take your pick.

Still, there was a garden to be planted — peas to be tucked into neat double rows, a trellis to be made for the future pea vines, corn to be hoed into hills, mounds to be created for the summer and winter squashes, and a couple of teepees to be lashed together from alder branches we had cut last fall for the pole beans.

The garden was my job. My husband Bob had built our home — almost single-handedly — out of spruce logs cut from the twenty acres of wooded property we had bought in the village of Pretty Marsh on Mount Desert Island, Maine, or to those who have to say it often, MDI.

Bob was a builder of small wooden boats, with his own

one-man company, RKL Boatworks. He had started out building a cedar wood-strip canoe for the family, but every time he took it out on the water, or even put it up on the roof of his truck, someone would stop him and ask where he'd gotten it. Eventually he started taking orders and expanding his repertoire to other small boats — dinghies, peabods (double enders), Rangley lake boats, sailing skiffs, and such. But the business was still young and the orders sporadic. In between the boat commissions, he took on house carpentry jobs. That's where he was this particular morning, finishing out an extension to a summer home. I was taking a couple of years off work to be a stay-at-home mom until our two children, Benjamin, almost six, and Alexandra, two-and-a-half, were both in school.

I wasn't, and am still not, an especially good gardener — my rows tend to be crooked and I'm never able to keep up with the weeds. But I do enjoy it, blackflies, mosquitoes, soggy springs and all, as a vital part of the rural life we chose when we decided to settle on Mount Desert Island. Also, I love dirt, the smell of moist soil, the feel of it in my hands. Mushrooms are just about my favorite food because I imagine they taste like dirt.

But on this unlovely day, thinking about having to go dig in that cold, wet dirt, I groaned. Alexandra, who had climbed into bed with me after Bob left for work, looked at me solemnly.

"French nice toast?" she asked — her version of "Would you like to make me some nice French toast?" Presumably, she felt that since such a breakfast treat always made her feel better it would make me feel better too.

It did sound pretty good. We had plenty of syrup, which we had tapped from our own maple trees last February and boiled off on our big old Queen Atlantic cast-iron cookstove in the kitchen. In a traditional plaster-walled house that would have been a big mistake — the plaster would have absorbed all the moisture from the constant steam and fallen out in chunks. That's why the big syrup outfits build special "sugar houses" for this process. But in our house, the only thing the logs absorbed was a faint maply scent that lasted throughout the "sugaring" season and a little beyond.

"French nice toast it is," I told my daughter, and we rolled out of bed and hustled into the warm bathroom to get

dressed. A big copper water tank stood in one corner of this, our only bathroom. The water was heated by the Queen Atlantic downstairs and bubbled up to the bathroom tank through slender coils of copper piping. We had no central heating, just the Queen Atlantic and a Jotul woodstove downstairs, and an enormous fireplace Bob had made from sea-polished popplestones we collected along the shore. But even on the coldest winter mornings, before we stoked up the Jotul, the bathroom was always warm and cozy. It was also big enough for the whole family to crowd into at once, including our 75-pound Alaskan malamute, Nahvoo (which, very appropriately, means beautiful in Inuit) who liked to be included in all family gatherings, wherever they occurred.

Benjamin was already up, playing some fantastic game in his room involving, as usual, spaceships. But he was easily lured away from whatever planet he was visiting and out of his PJs by the offer of French nice toast.

All in all, it was a normal morning in our household. There was nothing about the breakfast — the cleaning up, the brushing of teeth, tying of shoes and struggling into sweaters, the gathering up of garden tools and trooping out the back door to the newly tilled garden — to suggest that something totally unexpected was, in just a few minutes, going to enter the picture and change our lives.

I had just begun addressing a couple of dozen skinny green bamboo poles which, with a little weaving and twine, would become the trellis for our sugar snap peas, when the phone rang.

Drat! I considered ignoring it, but back then, before telemarketers hounded one throughout the day with promises of "fabulous prizes and deals of a lifetime," a phone call was usually from someone you actually might want to talk to.

"Watch your sister," I told Ben, and galloped back up to the house.

It was Bob.

"Nan," he said, sounding a bit breathless. "Get the kids and come on over here. I have something to show you."

Now here was something out of the ordinary. I couldn't recall Bob ever stopping work midmorning to invite his wife and kids to come over and have a look at his latest carpentry project. Oh, sometimes, on a nice day, we showed up for a picnic lunch. But this was neither lunchtime nor a nice day.

"What's up?" I asked.

But all he'd say was that it was a surprise.

Oh well, it sounded more interesting than bamboo pea poles, so after I hung up, I called to the kids who were worm

hunting with their trowels in the soft wet earth of the garden. There was a change of plans, I told them. We were going to visit Daddy at work. I didn't mention the surprise thing, in case it turned out to be some clever roof joist or fancy porch rail their father had devised. It's the sort of thing Bob could very well have gotten excited about, but not exactly a show-stopper for kids.

It only took about five minutes to drive, in our powder blue VW van, the few miles to the shorefront summer cottage where Bob was working. The property belonged to my relatives the McGifferts, and this place was one of the reasons I had been so keen to buy land for our own home here in Pretty Marsh, rather than on the other side of the Island, in Northeast Harbor, where I had spent my childhood summers, or in Southwest Harbor, where Bob's family vacationed.

Pretty Marsh, located on the Western fringe of MDI, is aptly named. The village, with its gently rolling landscape of hay meadows and evergreen, oak, birch, and maple forest, is divided in half by a loop of salt marsh that is connected at both ends to the sea. It began life as a quiet little farming and fishing village populated by some of the first settlers of MDI. Later it became an active sawmill town, where logs were cut into lumber and floated down the marsh to be loaded onto big sailing ships waiting in Pretty Marsh Harbor. During the mid-nineteenth century, the village boasted a fancy hotel where people like Hannibal Hamlin, President Abraham Lincoln's first vice president and a native Mainer, spent their off time. But it never really became a fashionable place, which probably saved it from the fate of Seal Harbor, another small village on the eastern edge of the Island, which is positively bristling with oversized summer homes built by such newly wealthy families as the Rockefellers, DuPonts and Edsel Fords (Martha Stewart now owns that one).

With the lumber mill and hotel long gone and their sites returned to woods or meadow, Pretty Marsh had become a quiet little village again. It is very, well, pretty.

When I was a girl, a couple of times during the season my parents would drive me and my four brothers and sisters over to Pretty Marsh to my Great Aunt and Uncle's summer cottage for tea and cookies. Their house sits on a narrow spit of land inside the greater harbor, which with Pirate's Point, another finger of land a few hundred yards across the water, forms its own small cove. Of course my brothers and sisters and I all loved the name "Pirate's Point" which suggested all sorts of scenarios for the games we played while the grownups chatted on the little apron of lawn facing the cove.

I loved everything about this place. The cozy gray-shingled cottage with two lilac bushes framing the front door was much smaller and far less formal than the great pile of a house where we spent our summers. Unlike most of the big summer cottages, the kitchen here was designed for a family, not servants, and the broad pine floors in the bedrooms were painted a brilliant aquamarine blue. It also had its own little telephone niche off the front hall, and all you had to do was pick up the receiver and the operator would come on the line. "Yes deah, what number you callin'?"

I loved the crunch of acorns underfoot as we traipsed down the narrow trail that meandered through an oak grove to the shore. I loved the long sweep of rocky beach, always a super place to find spiny sea urchins or nippy little green crabs to chase each other with, or pearly mussel shells and gooey, transparent jellyfish — also good for chasing. I loved the lucky stones (smooth beach rocks with a white ring around them) and the odd bit of sea-polished, pastel-colored glass, which I'd add to my collection.

Moored a little way out in the Harbor, in a pool of deep water, would be my cousins' little gaff-rigged sloop, the *Dirigo*, named for the Maine state motto, which means "I Lead." Sometimes my cousins would take us out for a sail. Depending on the wind's direction that day, we might tack back and forth from one shore to the other, to get out of the cove and into open water. Then we'd scream along on a reach through the Bartlett Narrows, with the water boiling up around us, heeling over so far that some of us had to sit on the windward rail to keep the boat from capsizing. Then, with the prevailing breeze at our back, we'd run before the wind on the homeward journey, our silk spinnaker bellying out over the bow like a giant balloon. Oh it was grand! And if we were lucky — and most often we were — we'd see a school of porpoises threading through the water like giant black darning needles, or a minke whale, or a harbor seal or two popping its head out of the water. Sometimes, dozens of them lolled about on the ledges that appeared at low tide, looking like a bunch of fat old men dozing on the beach. On one of those

Dirigo excursions, as we sailed into the entrance of the cove, I saw a pure white seal pup perched on a small ledge. It was the first time I'd come upon one so close and out of the water. It looked like the Little Mermaid statue in Copenhagen Harbor that I had seen in picture books. But this, I thought, was a real mermaid. I saw it watching us as the wind blew us by. After that, I looked for the white seal every time we sailed there, but I never saw it again. I've learned since that while harbor seals are usually born with the markings they will bear the rest of their lives — which are quite varied, everything from reddish brown to big black-and-white splotches — a few are born with a pure white fur called lanugo, which they shed in just a few months. So I may very well have seen that seal again, only by that time it had changed its spots.

The house would be empty now. My Great Uncle Cush and Aunt Elisabeth and the entourage of cousins wouldn't start arriving for another month or so, and the *Dirigo*, or one of its successors, was still at the boatyard waiting to be launched for another season of sailing. Still, as we drove down the long, bumpy driveway, through the dark tangle of woods that always seemed on the verge of swallowing us up, I felt the same sense of happy anticipation I had as a child.

Nahvoo, who often accompanied Bob to work, greeted us when we pulled up to the cottage. She was not usually an excitable sort of dog. She rarely barked, and normally greeted strangers and unusual circumstances with a quiet, wolflike dignity. But she seemed rather agitated now, prancing nervously about the children and emitting odd little woofs.

When Bob came around the corner of the house, she became even more excited and noisy, and he suggested we leave her in the van while he took us to see the big "surprise." Nahvoo was not pleased. Her muffled howls followed us as we all trooped after Bob, down the familiar path through the oak grove, *crunch crunch* over the acorns, and down to the shore.

"What is it, Bob, what is it?" Ben kept asking his father, but only got "You'll see," as a response. Benjamin, by the way, started calling Bob and me by our first names as soon as he heard other adults doing so, abandoning "Mama" and "Papa" along with the rest of his baby talk. We tried to convince him to use something a little more intimate, like "Mom," or "Dad," maybe, but he was a serious little boy, and in the end, we were just grateful he didn't address us as Mr. and Mrs. Lincoln.

Alexandra was thoroughly absorbed in the task of gathering acorns along the way, as if the opportunity to collect a pocketful of these was reason enough for such an unexpected excursion. Above us, the leaves on the oak trees were just beginning to burst their pale green buds. Not as big as a mouse's ear yet, which, as local lore has it, is the time to plant corn. Thinking of the garden I had so readily deserted, I made a mental note to hold off on the corn.

We reached the end of the path and clambered down the short, steep bank to the rocky beach. At first I didn't notice anything out of the ordinary — except maybe that the cove was empty of boats, and the fog was so thick I couldn't see the opposite shore. It was a very low tide, so there was a lot of beach to scour for whatever Bob wanted us to see.

I was just about to give up in exasperation and demand that Bob tell us what the heck we were supposed to be looking for, when I saw something move about fifteen or twenty feet ahead, halfway between the water and the high-tide line. I walked toward it, squinting myopically — I'd left my glasses in the car. Ben and Alexandra followed, uncharacteristically quiet, each holding one of their father's hands.

The thing moved again as we approached, and I could see that it was trying to wedge itself under a large barnacle- and seaweed-covered boulder. Then it lifted a dark, wet little head, turned toward us and cried out, making a weak and mournful whooping sound.

"There's my little kitty!" Alexandra announced gleefully, using her name for any furry animal she couldn't immediately identify. Pulling free of her dad's hand, she toddled at full tilt down the beach.

I caught her on the fly. "No, sweetie," I said, holding her close. "It's not a kitty, it's a little baby harbor seal. And we shouldn't go any nearer. We don't want to frighten it, or frighten its mama away."

In fact, I was pretty sure we should immediately leave the area, in case the mother seal was somewhere out there in the cove, anxious to get to her baby, but too afraid to come ashore because of us.

Still, something seemed terribly wrong with this little seal's predicament. In all my years of harbor seal spotting, I had never seen a pup left alone on this or any other populated shore on MDI. I had seen them sunning themselves on the rocky reefs outside the harbor at low tide, and at sea, but the sight of this forlorn-looking little thing hiding beneath its boulder, totally alone and unprotected, didn't seem right at all.

Bob told me that it had been Nahvoo who'd found the pup. Confused about what the thing was, she had set up a racket of barking that eventually brought Bob down to the beach to see what was the matter with her. If Nahvoo had been a fox or coyote, or even a different, more predatory sort of dog, the pup wouldn't have stood a chance. Which is why it seemed doubtful its mother had meant to leave it there — but who's to say there can't be foolish mothers in the wild?

As Alexandra had, all I wanted to do at that moment was run to the pup, gather it up in my arms, and carry it away to a safe warm place — home, for instance.

But, darn it, Bob and I knew better. Instead, we let the children look at the little animal for a minute more, then shepherded them back to the path and up to the house.

"Can we have it, Nan?" Benjamin asked on the way up the trail. "Can we take it home? It needs us."

"I don't think so," I said, giving him a sideways hug. "The mother seal will probably return for it when the tide comes in a bit."

"But what if she doesn't," he pressed. His big blue eyes filled with tears. "We can't just leave it there."

I didn't have an answer for him. Because, frankly, I totally agreed. If the mother didn't come for the pup, there was no way on earth I was going to leave it on the beach, any more than I would leave a human child lost and crying on a dangerous street corner.

The seal pup's welfare was not my call, however. The management of Maine's wild animals comes under the jurisdiction of the state's Fish and Wildlife Department. One can't just snatch a baby wild animal — be it seal, raccoon, squirrel, fox kit, or whatever — to take home on a whim, or worse to sell as an unusual pet. At least, not any more you can't.

A long-forgotten memory popped into my head.

When I was child coming onto MDI at the start of the season, every year we'd pass the same hand-painted sign. Set in front of a dilapidated farmhouse near the head of the Island, the sign read "Seal Pups for Sale" in big red drippy letters.

Every year, remembering the little white seal, I begged my parents to stop and buy me one. Despite some near tantrums on my part, they never did. But then one year the sign was gone. Probably, it was around the time when the state first began to crack down on such trade. Those baby seals, I now realized, had probably been snatched from the rocks or the water while their mothers were fishing. It was likely they hadn't survived for more than a couple days, perhaps breaking the heart of some other little girl more persuasive with her parents than I had been.

Without question, the best thing for this little pup would be for its mother to return and take it back out to sea where it belonged. But Benjamin's big "if" was impossible to ignore. Surely, I thought, there was some agency or shelter that rescued abandoned or injured wild animals.

Bob and I decided we should call the Wildlife Department. While I made the phone call back at the house — I had to dial the numbers directly myself now — Bob returned to the path above the shore to keep watch on the pup from a safe distance. The tide had started to come in, and we thought that maybe when it reached the boulder, the pup would slip into the water and go look for its mother on its own. If that happened, all we could do was wish it well. Like the memory of the white seal, this encounter would be added to a lifetime of memories and family history on Mount Desert Island.

Chapter Two

MDI is a large heart-shaped — or as some prefer, lobster-claw-shaped — island off the central coast of Maine, about three hours Down East of Portland. The rather directionally muddled term "Down East" refers to the entire coast of Maine as one travels north. The farther north you travel, the farther Down East you're going. The term is derived from the old sailing ships, called coasters, that used to ply the Atlantic Coast from New York City to Eastport, Maine, carrying ice, lumber, and granite for the big-city buildings, cobblestones (we Down Easters call them popplestones) to pave the streets, and whale oil to light the lamps. With the prevailing winds coming out of the southwest, to travel northeasterly up the Maine Coast these multi-masted schooners would have to sail downwind — go "Down East."

In the early twentieth century, when my grandmother was just a girl, she came here with her family from Boston every summer. They reached MDI by taking a train to Rockland and traveling the rest of the way by steamboat — the *J.T. Morse*, usually. Nowadays, people still come here by boat, everything from sailing and motor yachts to thousand-foot cruise ships such as the *QE2*. These all find safe harbor in several deepwater pockets stitched into the ragged forty-mile circumference of the Island. But you can reach it by a bridge, too, which spans a short distance across the shallow Mount Desert Narrows.

In addition to its harbors, the Island has about a dozen mountains. Well, some of them are really just hills, but we like to call them mountains. Cadillac Mountain is the largest at about 1,500 feet, and although some Eastporters and Nantucketers argue this point, it is the first place in the United States to be touched by the sunrise. It was these granite-topped mountains, scraped bare by the passing glaciers of the last ice age, that prompted French explorer Samuel de Champlain to name the place *Isle des Monts-Deserts* — Island of Deserted Mountains — when he first sailed into view some four hundred years ago. The Island also has miles and miles of dramatic coastline, three beautiful lakes, and Somes Sound, the only true fjord on the Eastern Seaboard, which almost bisects the island and gives it its distinctive shape.

When Champlain sailed by in 1604, the Island was indeed uninhabited, but not deserted. Various Indian tribes of the early Abnaki nation would arrive by canoe during the summer months to throw big clambakes on the shore and collect sweet grass in the salt marshes for their baskets. Their descendants, the Maliseets, Penobscot, Passamaquoddy, and Micmacs still come down from the Indian Island Reservation, near Bangor, for the sweet grass. When I was a girl, they went door-to-door selling their beautiful basketry. Now those baskets, which seemed expensive back then at $10 or $15 a pop, are now museum pieces housed at the very impressive Abbe Museum in Bar Harbor, which has the largest collection in

the country of Northeastern Native American arts and arti-facts. And the new ones sell for $100 or more — much more.

One summer, when I was a young woman of nineteen, I was invited by a young man whom I had met at a dance to go on a dig at one of the shell heaps left by these early summer visitors. This was at a place called Fernald Point, near the mouth of Somes Sound. It turned out to be one of the most interesting dates I'd ever been on. For one thing, I loved archaeology, and sifting through the brittle layers of ancient clamshells for treasures — a pot sherd, or arrowhead, maybe —

was definitely my idea of a good time. For another, my date had brought a friend along, a lanky, good-looking guy named Bob Lincoln. That afternoon my date found a bear claw with a little hole drilled through the top, and Bob and I found each other. Of course, such unscientific archeological digs are frowned upon now, as is, I suppose, falling for you date's best friend. But we were young and couldn't help ourselves.

Fernald Point was also the site of the first attempted settlement by Europeans on the Island in the early seventeenth century. But after just a few months, the unfortunate little band of French Jesuit priests was literally blasted out of the place by an English warship.

The first settlers of European stock to successfully build permanent homes on the island, in the mid-eighteenth century, were fisherman who harvested the abundance of cod, mackerel, halibut, flounder, and herring, using hand lines, nets, and purse seines. Lobsters, which were considered to be about as desirable eating as cockroaches, didn't become popular until the nineteenth century — perhaps when someone decided to try one with melted butter. Now lobstering is by far the biggest commercial fishing industry in Maine, although some oldtimers still refer to them as "bugs."

The fishermen were followed by farmers who cleared acres of trees and rocks to create fields for hay, potatoes, and other crops, and to graze their dairy cows and horses.

The next big wave of summer visitors were the society nobs from Boston, New York, and Main Line Philadelphia, who were drawn here by the gorgeous landscape paintings of

Frederick Church, Childe Hassam, Thomas Cole, and other popular artists who camped out — or "rusticated" — on MDI in the mid-nineteenth century.

These wealthy visitors stayed at increasingly gargantuan hotels built for them in towns all over the Island, but most of all in Eden, the Island's biggest town, later called Bar Harbor. Eventually, they started buying up shorefront and hilltop properties, with their magnificent ocean views, with an eye to erecting their own mansions — or as they were preciously termed, "cottages." These homes had names like *Sonagee, Breakwater, Mizzentop, Reef Point, Keewaydin* and *Chatwood*, and most were staffed by large retinues of uniformed servants, and supported stables of perfectly matched carriage horses, which the owners liked to parade down the main streets of town, hoping to be the envy of their neighbors. Bar Harbor was so popular with the international high society set that in its heyday it was nicknamed "Little Paris."

In 1919, the country's first privately endowed park was established on MDI to preserve the Island's most beautiful vistas from further development. Originally named Lafayette National Park it was later changed to Acadia.

If you do any serious hiking or climbing on MDI, you are bound to come across a number of bronze plaques hammered into the granite at mountainsides, mountaintops and cliff faces. Three of these plaques are dedicated to the founders of Acadia National Park. One of them was my great-great grandfather Charles W. Eliot, who was then the president of Harvard University. His plaque is on the summit of what used to be called Asticou Mountain, but was later named Eliot Mountain in his honor — although my somewhat reactionary family still refers to it as Asticou.

In the late nineteenth century, C.W.'s son Charles used to bring a gang of his fellow Harvard undergraduates, including his younger brother, my great-grandfather, Samuel Atkins Eliot, up to the Island every summer to camp out at Fernald Point — the same place I met Bob over the shell heaps — and other open spaces along the Sound. The boys would scour the shores, sail along the coast in the Eliots' boat, the *Sunshine*, and bushwhack up the mountains and through the woods (there were no trails then) in search of interesting flora, fauna, and marine life. At the end of each day's excursion, they would write the details down in their journals. They called themselves the Champlain Society, and they kept up this annual camping expedition for six years.

Charles eventually convinced his father to build a summer home at Northeast Harbor. The house C.W. built at the base of Asticou Mountain, facing Bear Island and the Western Way beyond, was one of the first summer homes on that side of the Island. After young Charles graduated from Harvard, he became a landscape architect with Frederick Law Olmstead's firm. In addition to helping design the "Emerald Necklace" in Boston, a swathe of parkland framing the city, he was particularly interested in preserving the beauty of Mount Desert Island. He had just begun devising a plan, or at least suggesting that there should be a plan for a park here, when he died of meningitis in 1897. He was only thirty-seven years old. His grieving elderly father picked up the banner, and with the help of John D. Rockefeller, Jr., who had the money to buy large tracts of land, and George Dorr, who had the youth and energy to do the foot work, completed what his son had started.

The park is now a patchwork of near-wilderness areas neatly fitted between the Island's towns and fishing villages and embroidered with hiking trails and carriage roads — built by Mr. Rockefeller for all those folks with the fancy horses. Horses and carriages still trot along these packed-dirt roadways, which girdle several of the Island's mountains and lakes.

Like me, Bob was a descendant of the third wave of summer visitors. Not the fabulously wealthy Bar Harbor set, but a more modest breed of proper Bostonians who erected big, but sensible "cottages" with nice views of the water in the smaller towns — my family in Northeast Harbor at Asticou Foreside, and Bob's across the Sound in Southwest Harbor at Spruce Bough. We both spent our childhood summers on the Island and dreamed about one day not having to leave come September. When we got married, we talked about how we would live, work, and raise our children year round on MDI.

We had no idea how we would do it, neither of us having any apparent skills at fishing, or any of the other traditional trades of native islanders. But who says dreams should be logical?

Soon after we married, Bob had to go into the Armed Services. For most of his tour of duty, we were stationed in Anchorage, Alaska, where he trained with the Olympic Biathlon squad and instructed the snow troops in skiing and sharp-shooting.

We loved Alaska, and even considered trading our Island

dreams for life on the edge of the country's most vast wilderness. Everything in Alaska seemed vast — built to a bigger and grander scale than in our native New England. The mountains were taller and far more commanding, the forests thicker, the bald eagles more prevalent, the moose, bears, and fish bigger. Even the moon looked three times as big when it rose over those jagged snow-capped peaks that loomed over Anchorage. Still, in the end, we missed the gentler, more accessible mountains of Mount Desert Island, the pink granite cliffs along its coast, and the little outer islands scattered like leftover puzzle pieces in the sparkling green waters of Blue Hill and Frenchman Bays and the Western Way.

What's more, while living in Alaska Bob discovered he did have a talent that would make it possible for us pursue a life on MDI. He could build things.

When I was pregnant with our first child, Bob used the well-equipped craft shops at Fort Richardson to build a beautiful black walnut cradle and several other handsome pieces of furniture. He was a natural.

Mount Desert Island has an extensive boat-building industry, everything from sturdy working-class lobster boats to the world-famous motor and sailing yachts constructed at Hinckley Boat Yard. We figured there was enough boat-making and house-building going on all over the Island to keep Bob gainfully employed. I had no such skill, however, and imagined that I would supplement our income with waitressing, bartending, and any other job that left my days free to be a mom.

But we took a little of Alaska with us when we left. A big frisky

Alaskan malamute puppy and a big idea for our future home.

In our Alaskan travels, we'd become impressed with the hand-built log homes we'd seen. Really big houses, not the cute little cabins we'd noticed tucked away in the woods at various ski resorts or along rural roads in the East, nor the now popular kit-built log homes. These were two-story buildings, with wings, ells, walk-in fieldstone fireplaces, and wrap-around porches. Bob had always wanted to build his own home one day, and felt sure he could master this type of construction. So while living in a cramped, army-housing duplex at Fort Richardson in Anchorage, Bob and I first started planning for the big Alaskan-style log home he would build when we returned to Maine and Mount Desert Island.

I was newly pregnant with Alexandra when Bob started cutting the logs on our Pretty Marsh property, which we had bought a few months after he got out of the service. Most of our acreage was taken up by a heath (locally pronounced "hayth"), a low-growth, tundra-like area that reminded us of some of the Alaskan landscape. But on the edges of the heath there were still plenty of tall spruce trees for the house. Once they were felled, we had a lovely view of Sargent Mountain, the Island's second largest and my favorite to climb. It has an incredible deepwater pond at the top for the most delicious swimming you could imagine after a two-hour hike, and on the other side there is a teahouse, Jordan Pond House, that serves popovers and homemade ice cream. Also delicious, especially the peach.

While I couldn't help with the heavy work of tree-cutting

and dragging, I could remove the bark by straddling a log and shaving one long vertical strip off with a tool called a draw-shave. If you cut the logs in spring when the sap is still running, the rest of the bark comes off just like a banana peel.

After the logs had dried, or "seasoned," for a couple of months, Bob began notching the ends and stacking them on the cement foundation like, well, like Lincoln Logs, that toy construction set for children. When each level, or "course," of logs was firmly spiked in place, I was able to help again by caulking the cracks between the logs, using a creosote-soaked twine called oakum and any old rags we had lying around. I remember tamping into the cracks of what would be our bedroom a square of yellow cotton fabric with a design of little red flowers on it. It was the remnant of the Bonwit Teller sundress I had worn on one of our first dates.

Bob had worked out a sort of Rube Goldberg contraption with ropes and pulleys to lift the logs for the second floor courses, but sometimes he needed an extra set of strong arms. When he couldn't find a friend to pitch in, he cruised the roads in his battered old Ford pickup truck looking for burly hitchhikers.

"Sure I'll take you where you want to go," he'd tell them. "But there's something I want you to do for me first." Then before he got a punch in the jaw, he'd quickly explain the situation. Most of the time, these shanghaied travelers were glad to help out, and I don't believe Bob ever got hit.

Occasionally, as my pregnancy advanced and I desperately needed a break from an active three-year-old, Bob would take Benjamin with him to the house site to "help." A rookie being called up to the Major Leagues couldn't have been more ecstatic than our Ben when his dad asked him to come along. I remember his best friend, Max, calling him up to come over and play on one of those days, and overhearing Ben say, "No I'm sorry, Max, actually I don't play anymore, I only work."

Another favorite memory of that time is of Bob straddling the roof, with a masonry book in one hand and a stone in the other, and capping off the chimney, learning as he went.

We moved into the two-story, four-bedroom log house on Thanksgiving Day, when Alexandra was almost a year old. Local folks, who had never seen a log home of this size, called it the Ponderosa. For Bob and me it was heaven. We sometimes referred to it as Shangri-Log — but only between ourselves.

Chapter Three

The game warden I got on the phone listened patiently while I explained the situation with the seal pup.

"I know you're not supposed to interfere with these pups, Officer, uh, Warden," I said in the sort of breathless and urgent manner I might have used to report an automobile accident. "But honestly, this can't be right, the pup is obviously distressed, and why would the mother leave it in such a dangerous place. I mean, why would she?"

When I finished, the warden calmly explained that while it was indeed unusual for a mother seal to leave her pup on a mainland shore, it was not unknown. Most likely she would return on the incoming tide. But in any case, we should not do anything and continue to keep our distance until at least a full tide change had been completed — six hours away. If the mother had not returned by then, he said, we should call him back, and he would make arrangements for someone to come and see if the pup looked like it really needed rescuing.

"But you know they don't have much luck with them," the game warden said. "A lot of the pups are sick to begin with, which is why they were probably abandoned. And even the healthy ones rarely survive. It's hard to feed them without resorting to sticking tubes down their throats. They just don't thrive. It might be kinder to let nature take its course."

I knew the warden was just being honest with me, but leave that baby to slowly starve to death on my uncle's beach— or to get attacked by a fox, coyote or some other predator? Not likely.

"There's got to be some other way," I said. "Sometimes they live, don't they — what about Andre? How did he survive?"

I was referring to a very well-known Maine harbor seal, called Andre, who had been raised from a pup by a man named Harry Goodridge in Rockport, a fishing town a couple of hours down the coast from MDI. Not only had Andre survived, and thrived, he had grown up to be something of a 250-pound nuisance after he decided that the local fishermen's dories were the perfect thing to take a snooze in — often swamping them with his bulk. Eventually, Andre had to be penned in the summer, then carted off to the New England Aquarium every winter. Each spring he'd be taken down to Marblehead Harbor, an hour north of Boston Harbor, and set free to make his way — more than 200 miles Down East — to Rockport, which he did, unerringly, for the next twenty-five years, even when, in his dotage, Andre went blind.

"Well that's just the thing," the warden told me. "Andre was raised like a human baby in Harry's house, not in an aquarium. There's some who think that's the most successful method, because seals are pretty highly evolved animals and need real fostering, not just food. But who's got the time to take on that kind responsibility?"

I thought about the garden to be planted, two small children to be minded, meals to be cooked, and a household to be managed, before answering in about two seconds, "Maybe I could?"

The phone was silent for moment. "Well now, deah," the game warden finally responded. "If this pup does turn out to be abandoned, and you're really willing to take it on, I've heard there's a study being done up to COA where they're gettin' the students and volunteers to home-raise the pups to see if the survival rate improves and they can be returned to a wild colony afterward. If you're interested in participating, you should give 'em a call."

COA is the College of the Atlantic, located in Bar Harbor, which had undergone a few changes since its days as "Little Paris." After the two World Wars and a Depression, the town began to lose its glamorous luster. With the advent of air travel and the newly coined "Jet Set," people with money were traveling farther afield. Besides, it was hard finding enough servants to staff the huge estates that had been built in a more opulent and ostentatious era. In 1947, a forest fire destroyed dozens of these castle-sized cottages and left a charred landscape across a full one-third of the Island. With the Island's beauty deeply scarred, many of the surviving estates were donated to charities, or torn down as white elephants by families who found the taxes too high and the post-fire scenery too depressing. The fancy clothing, fur, and jewelry stores that had once lined the main street of the downtown, like a miniature Fifth Avenue, gave way to T-shirt emporiums and souvenir shops for the few day-tripping tourists who still came to see Acadia National Park.

In the past ten or fifteen years, however, Bar Harbor had been making something of comeback. Now that the blackened remnants of the fire had been overlain with new green growth, tourists were rediscovering the Island in droves, and a group of ecologically minded educators had decided to open an alternative college on the outskirts of town that focused on a curriculum they called Human Ecology — mankind's relationship to the environment, especially the marine environment. This brought more young people into the area, with their need for friendly coffee houses, bistros, nightclubs, and places to buy their books, sandals, anoraks, dashikis, and stone-washed jeans — the preferred uniform of the early COA student. Gradually, Bar Harbor was assuming the air of a college town.

The still-fledgling College of the Atlantic was housed in several of the surviving old mansions along the Bar Harbor shorefront, facing Frenchman Bay. In addition to its ecology courses, the faculty and students had begun important research on whales and other marine mammals of the North Atlantic. A young man named Steve Katona (who is now the president of a greatly expanded and more sophisticated COA) headed up that research program — called Allied Whale. Bob and I knew him slightly.

As soon as I finished talking to the warden, I called Steve at the college, and once again, but more calmly this time, explained what was going on. He pretty much reiterated what the game warden had said. Leave the pup alone for at least a tide change. If the mother didn't appear by then, call him, and

he'd send up a couple of volunteers from the college to check it out, and if they deemed it necessary, pick the pup up and bring it back to Allied Whale.

"We'll try to find a student or volunteer to take care of it," he said.

I took a deep breath and dove right in. "What about me?"

"Hmm." Steve hesitated for a moment. "That actually could be a possibility. But you should know that it's very hard to get these pups to feed, and if you do succeed, they have to be fed on demand, which is pretty constant, like a human infant. And even then they usually don't survive. I know you've got kids, Nan. Is this really something you want to put them through?"

It was a good point. How awful would it be for my children, not to mention myself, to bring the pup home only to watch it die?

I shook my head, erasing the thought. I simply was not going to let the pup die. "Yes," I said. "I believe we can all handle it."

During the rest of the conversation, Steve told me what I would need to buy for a formula for the pup, if it did turn out to be abandoned. He also gave me suggestions about where to keep it, how to get it to eat, what to watch for, and in general, as best he knew, how to care for it.

Like most people, I imagine, I assumed the pup would have to be kept in a bathtub full of water. We only had the one tub in the house — a huge cast-iron claw foot affair that actually would have made a splendid swimming pool for a small seal. But adding a seal to our usual morning bathroom brigade could have posed a major problem. So I was relieved when Steve reminded me that a harbor seal is furred mammal, like an otter, and did not have to be kept wet all the time as dolphins or whales do. He said that if we had a spare room in our house, which we did, we could keep it there.

"But you better get a couple of tarps to put down on the floor and take up any rugs you care about," he advised. "Seals can be pretty messy."

Hoo boy, what was I getting us into? I had just gotten Alexandra out of diapers. Now I might have to deal with seal poop?

At about this point, Bob interrupted with an update on the pup. Instead of slipping into the ocean as the tide rose, it was moving away from the water, scrabbling farther up the shore and taking shelter behind other rocks. Steve asked Bob to describe the pup. Was it fat and round, or thin-looking?

"It looks kind of like a stuffed toy that's lost a lot of its stuffing," Bob replied.

Bob's description did not sound good to Steve. He told me that a healthy, well-fed pup would be filled out like a fat little blimp. It was probably avoiding the water because it was cold, which suggested it hadn't eaten for a couple of days and was living off the insulating fat reserves it had been born with.

This, of course, broke my heart. Would it survive until high tide? Couldn't we go get it now?

Absolutely not, Steve said. Seal pups and their mothers have an uncanny ability to find one another, even when they are separated at birth. We had to give them every possible chance to be reunited before intervening.

Although I agreed to wait, I wasn't so sure anymore about this whole happy reunion thing. What sort of mother loses her baby at birth, lets it wash up on a dangerous shore, and then waltzes back after a couple of days to reclaim it? Who's to say she wouldn't lose it again, forget to feed it, or run off with a big handsome bull seal? Is that the sort of mother I wanted to raise my baby? Oops, I caught myself. This was not my baby yet. In fact, I already had two very antsy babies of my own, right here beside me, who were tired of listening to their mom talk on the phone. I'm sure they wanted to do something, anything, else.

I also knew it would be impossible for me to watch helplessly as the hungry pup crawled shivering up the beach, trying to escape the icy water for the next six hours. I had to do something else, too.

So I took the kids shopping. Bob agreed to check on the pup every twenty minutes or so, and I piled the kids and dog back into the van and drove to Somesville, the nearest town with a store. A.V. Higgins general store, a white clapboard building with a yellow and white striped awning facing Main Street, sat on an avenue lined with old elm and maple trees, lichen-spattered stone walls, and handsome white clapboard homes fronted by well-manicured lawns. This town is so darned attractive that during the summertime and leaf-peeping season, flocks of photographers arrive like starlings to snap pictures of its charming mill pond, arched wooden bridge, darling little library, and general store. As we trooped into the store, I made a mental note to visit the library across the street, and look for books about harbor seals.

As always, Vic Higgins was standing in back behind the meat counter in his white butcher's apron, while his wife, Ruby, waited at the checkout near the front door, a sharpened pencil behind her ear — she didn't trust adding machines and preferred to do the math by hand on a pad of paper. This elderly couple had been managing A.V. Higgins twelve hours a day, 365 days a year, since they'd bought the building a few years before World War II. I often stopped in here for a pound of hamburger, a quart of milk, light bulbs, a box of macaroni, dog food, or anything else I ran out of before I could make a trip to the supermarket in Bar Harbor. This time of year, wood-slatted bushel baskets filled with stiff slabs of dried salt cod lined the aisles, giving the store a pungent but not unpleasant odor.

I'm sure Vic and Ruby were curious about the strange purchases I made that day. A case of infant formula, three quarts of heavy cream, a bottle of liquid baby vitamins, another bottle of cod liver oil, and three plastic baby bottles with extra nipples. I also bought two large plastic tarps. All these things were on the list I had made while talking to Steve Katona. Being typical Down East Yankee types, neither Vic nor his wife would have dreamed of asking what the items I was buying were for, any more than they would inquire how my sex life was going. And since I still wasn't sure I would have any use for the stuff at all, I didn't say anything by way of explanation. Alexandra did prattle on about her new "kitty," however, and I just left it at that. Vic and Ruby must have wondered what sort of "kitty" we were feeding — a lion cub, maybe?

The next stop was the library. Like all the houses in Somesville, the library is a white clapboard building. It sits on a little rise of lawn beside a brook-fed mill pond. The overflow of the pond sluices over a dam into Somes Harbor, creating a constant miniature waterfall. In the nineteenth century, this area used to be the site of a boat-building industry. Great three-masted schooners were constructed here along the banks of the harbor — a deep side pocket tucked into the western edge of the Sound. When the hulls of the vessels were finished, the builders waited for the spring full-moon tide to slide them down a long wooden trestle, called "ways," and into the harbor to be rigged. Earlier in the town's history, a sawmill used the power generated by the mill-pond dam to turn the gears of its saws. The pond is no longer expected to earn its keep, though, and now Ruddy ducks, black ducks, and mallards find it a congenial spot to stop on their way to somewhere else and hunt for frogs and alewives. And just about every year, a pair of mallards will choose the reedy area along the banks of the brook across the road to raise their ducklings. In the summer, a sign is put up along the main road that runs between the brook and the mill pond to warn drivers to "make way for ducklings."

The library always had a good selection of recent fiction and children's books, and on rainy days it was a great place to take Benjamin and Alexandra to look for picture books to take home. But I discovered now that there was precious little about seals on the crowded shelves. Aside from the reference encyclopedia, I only found one slim book on marine mammals, with just a page or two devoted specifically to seals. I checked it out, and the kids picked out a couple of books, too.

When we got home, I made lunch, then let Benjamin and Alexandra help me roll up the braided rug in the spare room and lay down the tarps.

"You know, we're probably not going to need any of this," I reminded them. "We really do expect the mother seal to come back."

But I could tell they weren't buying it, and, in truth, I wasn't selling the concept that well, what with all these preparations.

"Won't it be lonely down here?" Ben asked, ignoring my disclaimer. "I wouldn't mind if it slept in my room."

"And mine!" Alexandra chimed in. "In the bed with me and Fuzzy Bear."

"Nope," I said. "This seal, if it comes to us, will need its own room. It will be up to all of us to make sure it doesn't get lonely." I paused a moment. How much should I tell them about the possibility of the pup dying? I crouched down and put an arm around each of them. "You know, guys," I said, "both the warden and Mr. Katona say there's a chance the pup won't survive no matter how hard we try to save it. Do you understand that?"

Alexandra nodded her head solemnly, not getting it at all, I was sure, just responding to the serious tone of my voice. But I could see Ben did understand, and then — he's very much like me — he shrugged off the thought and went back to smoothing any wrinkles and folds out of the tarp so that the pup, when it came, would be more comfortable.

This "spare room" was actually a small wing Bob intended to turn into a study one day, along with a darkroom for his photography, but it was now a sort of catch-all area, containing our freezer, a piano, a bed, and boxes of stuff I couldn't figure out where else to put. Of course, it never occurred to us that one of its incarnations would be a guest room for a seal.

After we finished getting the room ready, I checked my watch; about three hours had passed since the tide started coming in. At least three more hours to go. When Bob made his next call, he said that nothing had changed. The pup was still retreating from the advancing water, and the mother still had not come.

Not since I had been in labor with my own babies had I watched a clock so intently. And while there was no physical pain involved in this waiting, it definitely felt like labor.

I managed to get the kids down for a nap, then sat down to read what little information I had found in the library about harbor seals. It wasn't much, primarily dry facts and Latin terminology. I was informed that harbor seals, or *phoca vitalus*, literally "sea calf," are an earless *pinniped* found in the waters of all the northern oceans of the planet. They gather in colonies, mate at sea, and give birth, or "whelp," on rocky ledges called "rookeries." Harbor seals feed primarily on cod, hake, flounder, and other local fish. They molt their fur every summer and tend to migrate south to ice-free waters in the winter. That was about it. Then the book went on to discuss sea lions — the species you most often see performing in circuses. The author had a lot more to say about this eared variety of seals. Apparently, joining the circus is good publicity for *pinnipeds*.

So, like Bob straddling the roof of our house, I guessed I'd just have to learn as I went — but without the how-to book.

The weather had brightened a bit, so I decided to return to the garden. My heart was not in it, though, and the rows of peas, cabbages, and beets I'd planted that afternoon were even more crooked than usual. But it did eat up more of that terrible time. Another hour had passed when Ben and Alexandra woke up. Benjamin immediately asked about the seal pup, and I told him we were still waiting to see if its mom was going to come.

"It's been taking forever," he moaned. "We should bring it home now."

My sentiments exactly.

For the next interminable hour or so, the three of us tried to keep ourselves busy. I put together some sort of casserole for dinner; Ben occupied himself drawing the control panels for his spaceship on a big pad of paper, and Alexandra pushed herself around and around the fireplace that separated the kitchen from the living room on a wheel toy my mother had given Benjamin when he was about the same age — a stuffed Steiff seal.

When the phone finally rang, we all jumped. It was Bob. He said that there was still no sign of the mother, and the pup was quickly running out of beach.

I hadn't thought about that, but I remembered now that at high tide on the McGifferts' shore, there would be a only a narrow strip beach left before the steep bank into the woods. And on a full-moon high tide, sometimes there's no beach at all — the water comes right up to the bank. I had no idea what phase the moon was in that day, but was certain there was no way the pup could make it up that slope.

I called Steve.

"Look," I said. "The tide's almost full, the mother hasn't come, and the pup's in danger of being swept out into the harbor. What do you think?"

He hesitated a moment, then said the words I'd been aching to hear.

"I think you should go get it."

"Kids, get in the car!" I shouted, charging up the stairs to get a couple of beach towels from the linen closet. On the way out the front door, I spotted a pair of Bob's thick leather work gloves sitting on top of the mitten chest in the front hall. Did baby seals bite? I grabbed the gloves and raced out to the car.

When we got to the McGifferts', it was just as Bob had described. The tide had risen so high only about four feet of shoreline remained of the once-broad beach. The pup had taken its last refuge beside a large flat rock, which it was curled up beside, as if the unyielding, cold stone was the closest thing to a mother it could find. Bob and I took one last scan of the water to see if we could spot the head of seal looking anxiously toward the shore. Aside from a few bobbing lobster buoys, the harbor was empty. Even the few seaweed-draped ledges had disappeared beneath the tide.

We climbed down the bank, and I held the children's hands while Bob, taking one of the towels I had brought and wearing the leather gloves, advanced toward the pup. We did-n't know what to expect. Would it try to get away, struggle, bite? It did none of those things. Instead it raised its head, looked straight at Bob, and as he approached, let out a few explosive sneezes. But when he bent down, draped the towel over the pup and picked it up, it just lay quietly in his arms, too exhausted to put up a fight — or perhaps it was only relieved to be close to something warm and soft.

We walked slowly up the path to van. The kids, once again hushed by the awe of what was happening, climbed into the back seat. After I settled into the passenger seat, Bob placed the towel-wrapped pup in my arms. It fit perfectly, and felt very much like the first time the maternity room nurses had placed my newborn babies in my arms.

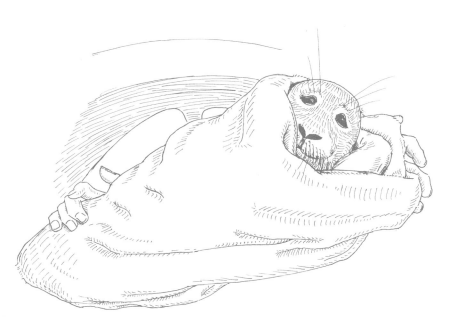

"It's all right, baby," I said softly, bending close to the dark, round head, which lay in the crook of my arm. "We're going to take care of you now."

"*Whoop! Whoop!*" the pup responded.

Chapter Four

Steve Katona said he would come by the house as soon as he got out of work, to check the pup for any obvious signs of sickness and bring some antibiotics. I suspected that he also wanted to see for himself if the pup was as starved-looking as Bob had described. I was worried about this, too. I hadn't gotten a really good look at the pup until now. Had we done the right thing? Maybe we should have waited longer. I ran my hand down the pup's side. Even through the towel, I could feel the bumpy ridge of its ribcage. That is definitely not a fat little blimp, I reassured myself.

When we got home, I carried the pup into the spare room, the floor of which was now covered with the two tarps, and gently placed it down. Now I needed to make up the formula. As I left the room, the pup tracked me with its big round black eyes.

In the kitchen, I poured two cans of infant formula and one quart of the heavy cream into a bowl, added two beaten egg yolks, two tablespoons of the cod liver oil, and an eye-dropper full of baby vitamins. Steve had explained to me that a mother seal's milk is almost entirely fat — hence the heavy cream. It is important for a newborn pup to gain weight very fast in order to withstand the frigid ocean water. The egg yolk would provide a little iron, and the cod liver oil would add protein and a "nice" fishy taste that would be more familiar to a baby seal than a grass-eating cow's milk. The plastic bottles, one pink, the other blue, were still warming in a pan of water on the stove when Steve drove up. He was a tall, bearish-looking sort of man, with long black hair and a full bushy beard to match; he resembled a lumberjack more than the stereotypical college professor.

The instant Steve saw the pup, which had managed to shrug itself out of the towel we had wrapped it in, he said, "Oh, yes. This is one hungry little guy." Then he rolled the pup onto its back and amended his statement. "One hungry little girl, I mean."

He said that she was probably no more than five days old, but should weigh a good deal more than the eighteen or so pounds he estimated her to be. Despite her thinness, she didn't seem have any of the obvious signs of seal distemper, parasites, wounds, or genetic abnormalities often found in abandoned pups, but he suggested I add the antibiotics to her formula, just in case she did have some infection.

The problem with feeding, he explained, is that a mother seal's nipples are retracted into grooves in her belly. So the nipple on a human baby bottle doesn't stimulate their sucking reflex. He suggested I make the holes in the nipple larger and try placing it in the crook of my elbow — recessing it.

Seemed simple enough. I was grateful for all Steve's help and advice, but now I was impatient to get on with it. I had two warm bottles of seal food ready to go and a very hungry pup in the other room.

Before Steve left, he wished me luck and told me that if it didn't work out, I could bring the pup into Allied Whale and they would try tube feeding her.

"Oh, I'm sure it will work out," I said with complete confidence, practically pushing him out the door. "I'm sure that won't be necessary."

Hadn't I successfully nursed two babies of my own? And, believe me, Benjamin had been no easy project. I never considered the possibility of failure — until about three hours later, when both the seal pup and I were covered from flipper to toe with fishy-smelling formula, and both crying, she from hunger, and me from frustration.

I had done exactly what Steve had suggested, but no matter how I placed the nipple — in the crook of my elbow, or the inside of my knee, between my fingers, my legs — I tried everything — she just didn't catch on. But she would hungrily suck the formula off if I poured it on my skin, which I'd been doing for the last three hours, though most of the concoction ended up in a puddle on the tarp. I had already gone through the first two bottles this way and was now on a third. Obviously, I couldn't get enough of the formula into her by that method. We were both exhausted, and her frantic whoops were getting weaker.

Steve had also cautioned me not to let her get overheated — in the wild, she'd be sleeping out on a barren rock in the middle of the ocean, not wrestling with some weeping woman in a warm log house. So I opened up all the windows to the cold night air. Now I was freezing as well, since I needed to keep the skin on my arms and legs bare to squirt the formula onto.

Or did I?

I found an old sweatshirt in a box of clothing headed for a yard sale, put it on and squirted formula onto the sleeve. The pup eagerly sucked it off. Hmm. Clearly it was the rubber nipple that was the problem. What else could I use to deliver the formula? I thought about cutting up the sweatshirt and jamming a piece into the top of the bottle to replace the nipple, but I was worried she'd inhale it. Anyway, the cloth didn't absorb that much of the thick liquid. What about a sponge? If I kept the ring cap on the bottle and put a wedge of sponge through the hole where the nipple should go, would that work?

I found a clean sponge in the kitchen, cut it into a triangle shape, and pushed it through the bottle cap, making sure the bottom of the sponge was too wide to be sucked through the hole and down her throat. Then I tipped the bottle upside down and squeezed, saturating the sponge with formula. When I sat down cross-legged on the floor next to the pup and offered my arm with the sponge protruding from my crooked elbow, she rallied once again and started to nuzzle my arm for more formula, coming closer and closer to the sponge.

Then she had it. In great powerful gulps, she started sucking the formula through the sponge. I almost screamed — actually, I think I did scream — when I saw the air bubbles streaming through the formula as she drained first that bottle and then another in a matter of minutes. As soon as she finished the second bottle, she rolled over onto her back, crossed her front flippers over her belly, and her eyes slapped shut.

For one horrible instant, I thought I had killed her. But, no, a deep, shuddering sigh and the rhythmic rise and fall of her chest reassured me that she had only fallen asleep, like any baby with a full tummy.

It had been almost five hours since the pup and I had started our battle with the bottle. About fourteen hours since

Bob's first "surprise" phone call. By the time I trudged upstairs, Bob had fed and bathed the kids, and they were all in bed asleep. I realized, somewhat guiltily, that in the last five hours I hadn't given a single thought to the rest of my family. When I bent down to kiss Ben good night, he woke up and wrinkled his nose. "Yuck, you smell like fish bait, Nan," he said.

"That, my darling, is the smell of success," I replied.

"Is the seal okay?" he asked.

"She's going to be fine," I said. "And by the way, her name is Cecily."

You'd think after a day that had turned out to be so eventful, and after a long hot bubble bath in that big old claw-foot tub — I was enormously grateful there was no seal occupying it — I would have popped off to sleep within seconds of climbing into bed. But the events of the day kept flickering in reruns behind my closed eyelids, along with a mental reorganization of my life around Cecily's needs — for how long? a few days, weeks, months? — seals can live up to thirty-five years — Yikes!

And there was something else. A familiar anxious feeling I hadn't experienced since Alexandra was an infant. Would I hear Cecily if she woke in the night, hungry again and frightened by her strange surroundings? What if she stopped breathing?

With that thought, I gave up, took an extra quilt, and went downstairs to sleep on the couch in the living room where I would be closer.

But first I checked on Cecily, who was still lying on her back with her flippers across her belly and sleeping soundly. I left the door open just a crack to make sure I'd hear if she started moving around.

I needn't have worried. About two hours later, I was catapulted out of a deep sleep, and almost off the couch, by a veritable chorus of *Whoop! Whoop! Whoop!*s coming from the spare room.

Before going to bed, I had made up two more bottles of formula and left them in a pan of water on the edge of the cookstove, where they would stay warm. I now took one of these and walked into the spare room, wondering if we would have to start the whole difficult process over again. As soon as she saw me, Cecily whooped a few more times, as if to say, "Hey, there you are! Where have you been? I'm hungry!" Steeling myself for the struggle to come, I sat down beside her and placed the sponge nipple in the crook of my elbow. No struggle at all! Cecily knew exactly what to do. She immediately latched onto the sponge and started nursing away, as if this arrangement was the most natural thing in the world. Smart, smart seal, I thought. As she gulped down the formula, I found I was able to gradually uncrook my left elbow and let that arm drop. When I moved the bottle closer to my body, Cecily followed. She finished curled up in my crossed legs, while I stroked her velvety soft fur with my free hand.

Now, for the first time, I was able to really study this marvelous little creature.

It's no wonder they call them pups. She did look like a

puppy, a Lab maybe, except that she had no floppy ears — no ears at all, in fact, just little dimples on the sides of her streamlined head. On either side of her perfect triangle of a nose sprouted about a dozen stiff, silvery whiskers; another set of whiskers sprouted above her eyes. The line of her mouth curved under each side of her muzzle in a permanent smile. The fur I was stroking was a dark, brownish gray, dappled with silver and black, graduating to creamy white on her underbelly. Her eyes were as big and round and black as marbles, but when I looked closely, I could see beneath their shiny surface a strange filigree of brownish coils. It startled me at first. Could this be right? Maybe she was blind, maybe that's why she got lost. Then I remembered the way she had tracked me when I left the room earlier, and how she had greeted me when she saw me come back. The coils, I decided, must have something to do with her underwater vision, which would be far more acute than her land vision. Her body was more torpedo than blimp-shaped, tapering from her large round head down to a narrow wedge formed by her back flippers. which, in repose, joined together like a pair of praying hands. Her front flippers were smaller, like little webbed wings, ending, like her hind flippers, in a set of five slightly curved claws.

One bottle was enough at this feeding. But after she finished, Cecily seemed perfectly content to let me hold her while she examined me with her nose and whiskers — snuffling eagerly through my hair when I bent down to her, nuzzling into my neck, along my shoulders and down my arms — virtually inhaling me. In the wild this is how she would have learned to recognize her mother. I can't have been anything like she was expecting, but she was willing to get to know me.

Eventually, she closed her eyes and fell asleep with a puppy-like sigh. But I held her for few moments longer, just liking how it felt to have an infant in my arms again. When I gently slid her onto the floor, she immediately rolled into what I would learn was her favorite sleeping position — belly up, flippers crossed.

I got another three hours of sleep before Cecily summoned me again.

When the rest of the family woke up the next morning, of course they all wanted to see Cecily. But she was still sleeping after her fifth bottle of the night, and I convinced them to have breakfast first, telling them she would let us know loud and clear when she was ready to receive visitors.

Sure enough, halfway through washing up — *Whoop! Whoop!* Both children stared at me wide-eyed. Was that our little seal making such a big racket? Alexandra wasn't quite so sure she wanted to see the monstrous-sounding creature anymore, but Benjamin was undaunted.

I opened the door. Cecily immediately recognized me and flip-flopped over to my feet, expecting me to assume the position we had worked out together. But when it was Benjamin who crouched down beside her instead and introduced himself ("Hi Cecily, I'm Ben"), she responded with a couple of those explosive sneezes we'd first heard on the beach when Bob went to pick her up — *Tchoo! Tchoo!* — and buried her head between my ankles. When Bob tried to pat her, same thing —

Tchoo! Tchoo! — with a couple of snorts and flipper slaps on the floor — *Smack! Smack!* — thrown in.

Alexandra, who had been lingering by the doorway, decided she wanted none of it, and went to look for the quieter, more congenial seal on wheels. Clearly these sneezes, snorts, and slaps were a warning. Keep away!

I felt badly for the children, and for Bob. They just wanted to be friends with the newest member of our family, but she wanted nothing to do with them.

"I guess she's still a little scared about everything," I said. "Let's give her some time to get used to us all."

But as I fed Cecily another bottle, while Bob occupied the kids, I wondered if she'd ever get used to the rest of my family. In the wild, a baby seal imprints totally on its mother, and under normal circumstances, they are practically inseparable from their mothers from the moment they are born until they are weaned. On a crowded rookery this bond is absolutely necessary for their survival. Cecily, it seemed, had imprinted on me.

This fact was further confirmed when I attempted to leave her, after she finished her morning bottle, to go see how Benjamin and Alexandra were doing. Instead of going to sleep, this time Cecily flip-flopped after me — pulling with her front flippers, then hunching her shoulders forward to get the rest of her body to follow, kind of like an inchworm. When I closed the door on her, she whooped and croaked piteously until I opened it again and let her follow me. *Flip-flop flip-flop* down the hall.

We're going to have to take up some more rugs, I thought.

Actually, it wasn't all that bad. Neither the seal poop situation, which wasn't that frequent or hard to clean up — especially if I slipped a mat under her when she wasn't moving — nor having a seal underfoot for almost all of her waking hours.

That first day, she hunched after me as I went about my household chores, draping herself across my feet whenever I stood still, and crying when she was hungry — about every two-and-a-half to three hours. It wasn't all that different from having a very needy child in tow. As long as I let her follow me about, she was happy and didn't make a fuss.

She was also perfectly prepared to follow me upstairs when I had to go to the bathroom, but I did have my limits. I put up our old baby gate again at the bottom of the stairs. Cecily punished me for this affront by whooping piteously from downstairs throughout my stay. Later, she learned to associate the sound of our pull-chain toilet flushing, and the rush of water down the pipes, with my imminent release from some mysterious prison, and would quietly wait for me to reappear on the stairs.

Other than that, during the day she had the run of the house — much to the distress of Nahvoo, who got a sneeze and a flipper slap in the face not only when she tried to approach Cecily to give her the customary doggy-sniff inspection, but every time she tried to approach me for a little attention.

The first time this happened, Cecily was lying quietly under the kitchen table at my feet, while I was reading a book and having a cup of coffee. Poor Nahvoo, not knowing that

danger lurked nearby, came over for a pat. Well, Cecily came flying out from under the table like a bat out of a cave, whacking away at Nahvoo's legs and snorting like an angry warthog. Nahvoo retreated in the face of this assault, and afterwards was careful to make sure Cecily was nowhere in sight before approaching me. This was another reason for keeping the upstairs a seal-free zone.

Over the following two days, Cecily did gradually learn to tolerate the presence of other family members with a bit more grace — the children, at least, she allowed to approach and pat her occasionally, although she never sought out their attentions. Benjamin seemed okay with her aloofness, and just got a kick watching her flopping about the house. By the third day, however, Alexandra started to show some signs of sibling rivalry whenever I fed Cecily in her presence — sucking her thumb more, or demanding a bottle, too, which was a little ironic since she'd been breast-fed. As I had with Benjamin when she was the new arrival, I tried to give Alexandra extra attention while Cecily was napping. And I must say, all in all, she handled the situation better than her brother had.

It was Bob Cecily couldn't stand, which seemed particularly unfair because he was the one responsible for her rescue. Whenever he came close, she sneezed and snorted at him and flopped away to find me. In the wild, a mature bull seal is not

welcome on the rookery where the pups are being whelped and nursed. Mating time comes later, after the kids are out of the bedroom, so to speak. A randy male can only be a danger to a small pup. Bob and I laughed over Cecily's apparent ability to recognize a randy male when she saw one, but still, I think her rudeness hurt his feelings just a bit.

The oak leaves had grown to mouse-ear size by now, and I managed to get in some more gardening, with Cecily hunching along after me as I hoed the hills for the corn. This made for one dirty little seal, and afterwards, I'd hose her down in the back yard, which she tolerated, but didn't seem to enjoy all that much. The blackflies were a problem though – perhaps they don't have a lot of these out on those reefs, or if they do, there's always the water to dive into to escape. Cecily didn't seem to have an efficient way of getting them off her face, so I had to constantly stop working to give her face a swipe with my hand.

One day, after a particularly dirty day of gardening – I think it had rained the night before, and Cecily was a complete mud-puppy – we decided to break the "No Seals Upstairs" rule. I lugged Cecily up the stairs, while Bob and the kids ran a tepid bath in the big tub. When it was about a foot deep, I plopped her in, and we all hovered over her watching to see what she'd do. She did nothing. She just lay there like a little crocodile with her face under the water. But she allowed me to wash her down, rolling her around in the tub until she was clean, and she seemed to like it better than being sprayed with a hose.

In the evening, when I'd stand at the stove cooking dinner, or at the counter chopping vegetables or kneading bread, Cecily would lie at my feet, one flipper curled possessively around an ankle. After tripping over her a half-dozen times, I eventually learned never to move without checking my feet first to see if there was a seal attached — even when Cecily was in the other room.

We got the feeding thing down pat, too. By the third or fourth day, I was able to replace the somewhat messy wedge of sponge with a rubber nipple and simply wrap a strip of sponge around it. At first, Cecily was somewhat flummoxed by the new apparatus, but she trusted me now and gave it a try. Eventually, I was able to omit the sponge altogether. On seven bottles, about 55 to 65 ounces of cream formula a day, she was gaining weight fast and beginning to look more like the desired blimp.

I could see us all going on like this indefinitely. I had even begun to house-train her and was making some progress. There was such a hullabaloo of activity when she did poop — me running to get paper towels, the kids exclaiming "Eeeyuuu!" and all the wiping up and cleaning her off — that it really seemed she was trying to wait until she was outside, or alone on the tarp in her room, before letting go. Once we got over this hurdle, I thought, and Cecily let us know when she had to go, like Nahvoo, well, life with a house seal would be a breeze.

I was, as much as possible, avoiding thinking about one extremely important fact: Cecily was a seal. Seals live in the ocean, not in log houses. They don't garden, they fish; they

don't bathe, they swim. And they really shouldn't need to be house-trained. I knew that at some point Steve was going to be calling to tell me it was time to reintroduce Cecily to the sea.

I dreaded that day. I was afraid that the moment I put her in the salty water, Cecily would suddenly remember she was a wild seal and disappear into the vast, cold ocean — a harsh and dangerous environment for which she was not yet equipped to survive.

Chapter Five

The call from Steve came toward the end of the first week. He said he would like to come by that evening to see if Cecily had put on enough fat to withstand the 52-degree ocean water. Looking down at the blimpy little shape draped over my feet, I knew the answer would be yes — and it was. Tomorrow would be the day for Cecily's first swim.

But where to take her? The long trek through the oak grove to the McGifferts' beach would be difficult — not to mention the steep bank. Bob and I discussed alternatives. Most of the shorefront property in Pretty Marsh is privately owned, and I doubted the owners would enjoy the sight of the Lincoln family and their seal trooping by big picture windows on their way to the water.

In the end, we decided to take her to the public boat landing at Pretty Marsh Harbor, less than a quarter-mile up the road from the McGifferts. Here you could drive a car right down to the shore. It wasn't ideal, because there was sometimes boat traffic in the area — maybe just a few lobster boats now, but later in the season, the harbor would be full of pleasure boats, many of them with sharp propellers. Oh God, did I really have to do this?

The next morning actually *was* one of those gorgeous

spring mornings the poets write about — a cloudless blue sky and enough of a warm breeze to scatter the blackflies. A lovely day for a swim. I'd hoped for a hurricane.

For the first time since we had rescued Cecily, she was going for a ride in the car. I had never taken her out on shopping trips or other errands that required a car, because I was worried the motion would alarm her — a surefire poop inducer — and also because I knew that as soon as I stepped out of the car, she'd start whooping like crazy, drawing the attention of passersby. Obviously, I couldn't have her flip-flopping after me down the aisles of the supermarket. So she stayed home, and I tried to time my trips during her naps.

After the kids were settled in the back seat, I lifted Cecily onto the floor in the middle of the van. She rolled over on her side to have a good look around. So far so good. But as soon as the car started, she scooted to the front to lie on top of my feet. Luckily, Bob was driving.

We parked the van on the launching ramp at the harbor and unloaded Cecily, who seemed perfectly fine after her ride. She looked about, not particularly interested in these new surroundings; but as always, she followed me when I started walking toward the water.

I was scared to death, but tried not to let Benjamin and Alexandra see how worried I was. I babbled on about what fun this would be for Cecily, and wasn't it just a magnificent day, and, oh, look at that pretty shell there. If I couldn't quite convince myself what a lark this all was, I did convince my daughter, who announced she wanted to go swimming, too.

"Ooh no, sweetie, it's much too cold for little girls," I said. "But perfect for a little seal with a fur coat."

Alexandra scowled and popped a thumb in her mouth, demonstrating that as far as she was concerned, a fur coat, like a baby bottle, was just one more thing I had neglected to provide her with.

We all stopped at the water's edge. Cecily put her nose into the ripples lapping across the pebbles, sneezed, and looked up at me. "Now what, mom?"

Well, she obviously wasn't going to make a mad dash for freedom.

I picked her up and walked into the water — sneakers and all — until it reached my knees. Good grief, it was cold! My legs ached in protest. When I plopped Cecily down into the water, she protested too, mightily. After splashing about frantically for a few seconds, she attempted to climb up my legs —

something her flippers weren't at all suited for. Gritting my teeth against the cold, I leaned down and held her sides, guiding her through the water as I had my own babies during their first swim. In a little while, Cecily calmed down enough to paddle with one fore-flipper in a tight clumsy circle around my legs, never completely losing contact with my skin with her other fore-flipper. After about a minute of this, I couldn't stand the cold anymore and waded back toward the shore as fast as I could. Cecily beat me out and was halfway to the car by the time I stepped onto dry land.

Okay, I revised my thinking. The problem wasn't what I would do if Cecily ran, or more aptly, swam away. The problem was, what was I going to do with a seal who was afraid of the sea?

We tried a couple more times that day, but with the same results. As long as I stayed in the water with her, Cecily would reluctantly agree to swim around my legs, but as soon as I made a move toward shore, she was out in a flash.

When I told Steve what was happening, he said to just give her time, eventually she'd figure it out. I wasn't so sure.

The following afternoon, after another session of forced hydrotherapy, I drove out to A.V. Higgins to get more cream. We were buying a lot of the stuff, and I finally explained to Vic and Ruby that I was feeding a baby seal. Ruby, adding up the prices on her pad of paper, remarked, "Well isn't that nice, deah." Vic just nodded.

On the way to and from the store, I passed a place on the road called Pond's End. This is where the Northern end of one of the Island's largest lakes, Long Pond, meets the road — a favorite swimming and boat-launching spot for us locals. I had taught Benjamin how to swim here and planned to continue lessons this summer with Alexandra, who was a true "water baby." It was also something of a ritual for me to finish a day of spring gardening — when I was covered in dirt, sweat, and blackfly bites — to jump in for a quick, refreshing swim.

Despite my less than stoic performance in the frigid harbor water, I am really no wuss when it comes to cold-water swimming. When my brothers and sisters and I were kids, my dad used to take us all out for a week of sailboat-cruising down the Maine Coast. He was a doctor, and it was the only way he could get a significant amount of time away from telephones — this was before cell phones, of course. Part of our cruising ritual was that all hands had to jump overboard every morning before we could have our breakfast. I grew to love the breathtaking shock of cold, and then the way my body gradually and painfully adjusted to the water's temperature. But that was in midsummer, when the ocean was several degrees warmer, and even then if you stayed in more than ten minutes or so, your body started to go numb as hypothermia set in. Getting out was best of all — I loved the tingly sensation all over my skin, as if I'd just bathed in champagne. I still love it.

There were no swimmers at Pond's End this day, and the water was still only a few degrees warmer than the ocean. But remembering Cecily's tranquil response to bathwater, I thought those few degrees might make all the difference — for both her and me.

When I got home, I called Steve and asked him if it would

be a bad thing to take Cecily swimming in the lake instead of the ocean. He thought about it for a while.

"I can't think of any reason not to," he said. "Harbor seals often swim up into rivers. But to be on the safe side, put her back in the salt water afterward in case there are any parasites in the fresh water she has no immunity to."

That afternoon, instead of going to the harbor, Cecily and I headed over to Pond's End. It was a weekend, and Bob had taken the kids and Nahvoo for a hike. By now, Cecily was a real pro when it came to riding in the van, and as long as I let her lie by my feet when I was driving, with one flipper lightly touching my gas-pedal foot, she was delighted to go for rides. I did wonder how I would explain this arrangement to a policeman if I ever got stopped, but I never did.

As usual, after I unloaded Cecily out of the car, she dutifully followed me to the water's edge. "Uh-oh, here we go again," I imagined her thinking. But instead of wading out to my knees, this time I plunged in head first — just as I used to dive off my dad's boat — and swam a little way underwater. When I came up for air, there was Cecily, nose-to-nose with me, and with an expression on her face that seemed to say, "Well it's about time, Mom, what took you so long?"

Now I watched in wonder as Cecily came into her own. The flippers that got her about on land so clumsily were transformed into wings. She flew through the water, executing belly rolls, flips, and loop-de-loops. She dove deep and skimmed along the bottom like a little submarine, nuzzling pebbles and my toes along the way, then she soared to the surface, exhaling

in a sparkling spray of fine mist. The circles she swam around me got wider and wider, and sometimes I lost sight of her altogether when she dove underwater, taking longer and longer to surface. I remembered Steve telling me that a harbor seal can stay submerged for up to half an hour. Yikes! It was one thing to lose a seal in the ocean, but what if I lost her in a lake?

I called her, "Cecilee!" In an instant, she popped up beside me, a silly grin on her face. "Come on, Mom, let's go, let's go!" she seemed to say as she dipped and bobbed around me. I swam with her for about twenty minutes before rolling onto my back to float, the warm sun on my face. As soon as Cecily surfaced and saw me floating, she stopped her cavorting, skimmed over to me, then climbed onto my stomach, laid her head on my shoulder, and fell promptly asleep.

Now I truly felt I had become a seal mother. I wished we could have stayed like that for hours, letting the water rock us to sleep together, just as her real mother would have done out on the ocean. But I was beginning to go numb. When I rolled her off me and headed to shore, she followed, this time reluctantly, making a few last belly rolls in the shallow water before climbing out and clumsily hunching her way back to the car.

That evening, when I took her to the harbor for her saltwater bath, Cecily needed no coaxing to enter. I was able to stand on the shore while she splashed and played and dove, constantly popping up to make sure I was still there watching, and, I imagine, wondering why I didn't join her. After a half hour or so, I called her in, and like an obedient child, she came.

A couple of days after Cecily's first swim, Steve phoned and suggested I introduce fish into her diet. Raw fish, of course. On my next stop to A.V. Higgins, in addition to the usual couple of quarts of cream, I added fresh smelts and herring to my shopping list.

"For the seal," I informed Vic Higgins as he wrapped up the fish.

"Yuh," he replied, and then in a burst of gregariousness added, "I'll save some out, if you like. Sometimes they go pretty fast when I get 'em in."

"That'd be great, Vic, thanks."

At home, I listened to my old Waring blender wheeze and growl as it ground up the concoction of whole smelts and cream I'd fed it. I was reminded of that classic old *Saturday Night Live* skit with Dan Akroyd hawking a machine called a Bass-O-Matic.

"Yes indeed folks, now you can make your own delicious bass frappés, right in your own kitchen!"

Well, I really could have used one of those things.

The finished product looked like whipped brain matter, peppered with little eyeballs, and it smelled disgusting. But Cecily thought it was yummy.

With the weather warming up, we were all spending less time in the house now — including Cecily. While I watched Alexandra play on her swing set, or worked in the garden, Cecily followed along, often rolling over on her back to take a snooze on the lawn. The bugs were still a problem, though, until one day, Bob thought of a solution — he built her a doghouse. Just a little one with a flap-screen door. Cecily learned very quickly to seek shelter from the blackflies and mosquitoes there, and she seemed to feel safe enough in her little house to allow me to leave her to go inside my own house without her following at my heels. I never left her out after dark, though, for fear of predators such as the coyotes that prowled in the woods and heath that surrounded our home. Some nights, I could hear them ululating at the moon, a cacophony of yips and howls. I had always loved the Sound, especially in the winter, because it made me feel as if I was living in the pages of a Tolstoy novel. But I didn't love it now. Now it meant danger, not romance.

Days, however, Cecily's swim time was divided pretty evenly between Long Pond and the Harbor.

The weather was turning out to be unusually hot for early June, and soon the lakewater had warmed enough for Bob and the kids to join Cecily and me in our daily swims. It was during these swims in Long Pond that Cecily revealed to the rest of my

family just how charming she could be. Where on land she had been awkward, nervous, and cantankerous around anyone but me, in the water she was an absolute party animal. Instead of behaving like an ill-tempered only child, she joined the family.

She loved swimming through legs, playing tag, slipping through arms, climbing on tummies or backs to hitch a free ride, and staging sneak shark attacks where she would disappear for minutes at a time and then suddenly reappear, spraying our faces with mist as she exhaled —*Brsshh!*

While Benjamin held onto her flippers, she would haul him along for a tow for a few yards before slipping his grasp. A dive to the bottom, and then, when he least expected it, she'd pop back up, always catching him by surprise. Cecily considered Alexandra, bobbing about in her orange life jacket, her own special pool toy — bumping her along through the water with her nose while her toy shrieked with laughter.

It took her a little longer to drop her caution with Bob and not dart off whenever he approached, but eventually, she let him join in the games, too. A small wooden float had been anchored offshore, and sometimes the five of us would haul ourselves up onto it, like a family of harbor seals, and bask in the sun for a while.

I was worried when other people started coming down to Pond's End to swim. How would Cecily react? Swim away, bite them? She tolerated them. She was content to allow other swimmers in same vicinity, but would skim away if they tried to become too familiar.

Usually, when people arrived and saw us all in the water, they assumed it was a remarkably aquatic dog we had swimming with us. Even when we were basking on the float, most assumed she was a puppy. It was so out-of-context; even though they were clearly seeing a seal, their minds said *dog*. It wasn't until we all trooped out of the water, with Cecily flip-flopping behind, that they were forced to believe their eyes.

"My Gawd, it's a bloody seal!" a man with a British accent exclaimed one afternoon as Cecily emerged from the water. I was tempted to tell him she was one of the rare, Maine fresh-water seals, but he looked too savvy to swallow that line. Instead, I explained what we were doing with a seal in a lake. Turned out he was the host of a British Broadcasting Company (BBC) afternoon radio talk show, and he ended up interviewing me on tape in his car, right there, while Cecily and the rest of the family splashed about in the water.

He asked me all sorts of questions about her care and feeding and, in general, what a day with a Cecily was like.

And I told him how, when she was ready, I would have to take her back to the colony where she was born and let her go. He asked me if it was going to be hard to give her up. "Ahh, that remains to be seen," I replied. "The care has been so intense, and she's become so attached to me, it's hard to think about all that ending."

"Will she be able to integrate with the wild seals out there?" he asked.

"We don't know," I said. "They've tried it with male pups, but when they reach maturity, it hasn't worked. They don't know how to fight, or any of the other male behavior they need to make a place for themselves — the tricks of the trade. But we think there's a good chance with Cecily because she's a female. All she needs to do to find a mate when she matures in three years is look sexy."

"Does it have to be good-bye?" he asked. "Or do you think you will ever see her again?"

"Oh I hope so," I replied. "I like to imagine that after she's found a mate and has had her pups, she'll come back to Pretty Marsh Harbor from time to time. I mean, I'd like to see my grandchildren."

The interview was fun — the host reminded me of David Frost, whom I loved, and since the program would only air in the UK, I wasn't worried that it would make the Lincoln house a local tourist attraction, or that more people would come down to the lake to see the amazing freshwater seal.

Chapter Six

When I took her to the harbor, Cecily was swimming farther and farther out to explore the water of Bartlett Narrows and beyond. Sometimes I would have to call and whistle for ten to twenty minutes before she finally agreed to come ashore. I felt badly having to interrupt her explorations before she was ready, but there was no help for it. My other obligations made it impossible for me to spend hours on the beach until my seal got tuckered out and ready to go home. I did have two other children who needed attention, too.

One morning, with all sorts of pressing errands to run and a birthday party to take Benjamin to, I decided to see what would happen if I didn't call her in — if I left her out there for a couple of hours and then came back to fetch her. Steve had suggested I try this to give Cecily more serious swim time. But up until now, I'd been ignoring the advice.

After feeding Cecily a morning bottle of cream o' fish, the kids and I took her down to the harbor as usual.

I explained to Benjamin and Alexandra what the plan was.

"Cecily needs to spend more time in the water learning to be a strong swimmer," I said. "I don't think she needs us to wait for her all the time anymore. So we'll just come back for her later, okay, guys?"

"But what if she gets lost and can't find her way back without us calling and whistling for her?" Ben asked, his brow furrowed with concern.

"That's not going to happen," I said. "Seals don't just use their eyes and ears to find their way home. They use their noses and their whiskers and their mouths. They can sort of taste and smell their way home."

This was the truth. When I had told Steve about seeing those coils underneath the surface of Cecily's eyes that first night, and how I had, for an instant, worried that she might be blind, he told me that a seal's keen sense of smell — which functions both in and out of the water — and the tactile sense of their whiskers are far more important to their survival than vision. Even the area around the nose can pick up stimuli from dissolved molecules in the water. This is how Andre was able to navigate hundreds of miles to find his way back home, even after he went blind.

In any case, my explanation seemed to reassure Benjamin. Meanwhile, Cecily was already halfway out of the harbor.

I drove off. It felt like leaving a child for her first day at school, and while I wasn't as concerned as Ben was about Cecily finding her way home, I was nervous that if she noticed I wasn't waiting for her on the beach, she'd turn around, come out of the water, and start heading down the road on her own in an attempt to find her mom. My brother had purportedly done this his first day of kindergarten.

I stopped the car just up the road, and we all watched. I could see her shiny little black head, moving swiftly out toward the Narrows, occasionally disappearing, then reappearing farther out. She hadn't noticed we were gone, so off we went.

I had intended to give Cecily and myself a couple of hours. Normally, when one of my children had a birthday party to attend, I stuck around — to help, and because I like kids' birthday parties. But after an hour and a half, I couldn't bear it any longer and asked the birthday boy's mom if I could leave her with one extra child, Alexandra, and take off for an hour. Ben seemed happy to see me go — I knew he was worried too — and Alexandra was so thrilled to be a member of her big brother's social set, she barely noticed my departure.

When I got back to the harbor, I walked out onto the pebbly shore with a baby bottle in hand and looked for Cecily's

shiny black head bobbing about amongst the boat moorings. There was no sign of her. I called and then called again. Still no Cecily. Uh-oh.

Out in the harbor, a group of lobstermen were rowing in from their fishing boat, coming in for a lunch break, I guessed. It was embarrassing, but I kept calling "Cecilee! Cecilee!" and waving the pink plastic baby bottle over my head. I planned to explain what the heck I was doing when they got to shore, but instead of rowing into the beach, they changed course and headed for the dock. They gave me a wide berth as they walked to their cars in the lot.

By the time Cecily's head finally popped out of the water about twenty yards offshore, the lobstermen were long gone.

This peculiar scenario would be repeated several times in the following days as I left Cecily out in the harbor for longer stretches. As far as I know, the lobstermen never saw her, and I've often wondered if the tale of the crazy lady with the baby bottle became a standard in their storytelling repertoire.

"Poor deah, probly lost a child at sea. Oh, I'm tellin' yuh, it was an awful pathetic sight."

But it wasn't their stories I was worried about. It was their propellers. More boats were being moored out in the harbor now, and Cecily had grown a little too accustomed to them for my comfort. Often I'd see her little head bobbing right next to a hull or stern. With her spending whole afternoons at sea, I needed to find a safer place for her to come into and wait until I arrived with her bottle and fetched her home.

As luck would have it, Benjamin had a playmate he had met at school named Jenny, whose parents, Jill and Steve Humphrey, and older sister, Christine — Chris — had recently moved into a lovely saltwater farm at the very end of the harbor. In fact, their shorefront connected with the McGifferts'. I'd met Jill a couple of times and knew she was studying to be a veterinarian. What could be more perfect?

I called Jill and asked if it would be possible to bring Cecily down to their shore in the mornings, then pick her up in the late afternoons. I promised to be as discreet as possible with a seal in tow. The Humphreys knew all about Cecily from Jenny, who often came over to play with Benjamin. They were happy to help.

It was, however, a good long way through a hay meadow from the Humphreys' big white farmhouse to the shore. Too long, I thought, for Cecily to negotiate on her own without getting overheated. And by now, she was far too big for me, or even Bob, to comfortably carry that kind of distance.

It was ten-year-old Chris Humphrey who solved the dilemma. When we arrived at the farmhouse, Chris was waiting for us with a big old wooden wheelbarrow.

I didn't know how Cecily would take to this new form of transportation. But once we loaded her up and started bumping down to the path toward the water, with Cecily facing forward, looking for all the world like the figurehead on an old sailing ship, she seemed to figure out exactly what was going on and began to whoop raucously, as if to say, "Faster, faster!"

I noticed right away that the water at this new spot was much warmer than in the harbor. At low tide, the Humphreys' shore was a wide expanse of mudflat, which would be warmed by the sun. When the tide came back in, it in turn would be warmed by the mud. I realized I could easily tolerate this ocean water for as long as I wanted. It had been getting crowded with boats and swimmers down at Pond's End, and with Cecily spending a great deal of her day at sea, we weren't swimming together as much, and I missed it. By the way she always encouraged me with impatient whoops to join her, before giving up and swimming off alone into the harbor, I imagined she missed those times, too.

Now we could resume our long swims together, in proper seal territory. It would be her turn to show me her world.

And she did. Cecily was a marvelous submarine tour guide, pointing out all sorts of fascinating things to see on the ocean floor: pebbles, shells, clumps of seaweed, mussel shoals, starfish, and scuttling crabs. I'd hold my breath for as long as I could and skim along beside her in the warm shallow water, dipping down to the bottom if she seemed particularly interested in showing me something up close.

If only I didn't have to surface every minute or so.

"What's wrong, Mom?" she seemed to say every time I came up for air. "This is great stuff I'm showing you here."

It *was* great stuff, and I wanted to see it all, but, darn it, I wasn't a seal. If I had been, I wouldn't have had to hold my breath at all. Steve had explained to me that seals can dive as deep as 200 feet. To withstand the pressures of such depths, they exhale all the air from their lungs before diving, depending on the oxygen stored in their blood and muscle tissue. While diving, their circulation is limited to the brain and other vital organs. Their heartbeat slows considerably — sometimes down to as much as one tenth of its normal rate. Their body temperature and metabolism are also reduced to save oxygen. Seals can swim as fast as eight miles an hour underwater. Clearly, I was cramping Cecily's style. But then I had an idea I thought might make us a little more compatible at sea.

I'd never done any scuba diving, and besides, we couldn't afford to buy the required equipment. But I had done a lot of snorkeling and loved it. You could buy a snorkel and face mask for less than ten bucks. One morning, before taking Cecily down to the Humphreys', I made a quick trip to Brown's Store in Bar Harbor, where they sold everything from aspirin to model airplanes, including snorkel gear.

I was so excited as we bumped down the meadow that day, Cecily as ever riding shotgun in the wheelbarrow and whooping with glee. I imagined hours of underwater play with her and finally having the chance to watch her in underwater action, unblurred, and without the constant interruptions for breathing.

Cecily, as always, took off like a shot as soon as we hit the water. I slipped on the face mask, bit down on the snorkel, and followed.

Oh, it was great. Now I could see everything in sharp definition, the colors, the contours, the way the sunlight rippled over the flats. I even liked the way my breath sounded coming through the hollow snorkel tube. If I wanted to see something on the bottom up close, all I had to do was dive down, check it out, and then rise just enough for the snorkel head to break the surface. I could resume my breathing without ever having to lift my face out of the water. Perfect! Up ahead, I could clearly make out Cecily's waggling bottom.

She turned, as she always did, to see if I was following. If it's possible to see a seal do a double-take, then I saw one at that moment. Cecily stared at me for a split second, shook her head, and stared again, her eyes widening — then, like a torpedo shot, she headed straight for me. I thought she was thrilled to see me with my face still in the water and was coming over to congratulate me. That is, until she crashed face first and full speed into my face mask, knocking the snorkel out of my mouth.

"Ow! Cecily," I yelled, pulling the snorkel gear off my head. "What the hell was that for?" But Cecily wasn't listening. She was too busy attacking the mask and snorkel still in my hand, butting them with her nose, slapping them with her front flippers, and sneezing at them.

Now I understood. When she'd looked back, expecting to see her usual mom, what she saw instead was a horrible one-eyed, tube-breathing monster that had somehow attached itself to her mom's body. So she attacked it.

I tried again, this time making sure Cecily saw me putting the gear over my face. But no way. As soon as I dove underwater she was at me again, batting, butting, and slapping at the mask.

Thus ended my brilliant idea.

Still, we continued to enjoy our swims together. I tried to join her on every reasonable day and brought the kids along on the really good days, although they preferred the warmer lakewater.

As long as I stayed in the water, Cecily stuck close by, making little forays out into the cove, then darting back when I declined to follow. She must have thought she had a terribly inept mother — I couldn't stay underwater for more than a minute, and for some reason, wouldn't join in her in the open sea. And by her standards, I was a pretty lousy swimmer, to boot. Perhaps that's why she stayed so close, in case I started to do something really stupid, like drown. Perhaps in this environment, where I was so obviously out of my element, she felt she needed to take care of *me*.

Only when she saw me safely on shore did she venture out into the cove, alone, to continue her exploration of Bartlett Narrows and, I presumed, beyond. With the Humphreys keeping an eye out for her, I didn't worry so much about her either, and so she spent most of the day now at sea. My daily life started to go back to pre-seal-pup normalcy. I missed her in the garden, hunching after me through the house, and the light touch of her flipper on my foot when I drove. But I have to admit life was a lot less complicated.

Before dark, I would return to the Humphreys' shore and whistle and call for her. "*Cecilee!*"

She would invariably appear in five or ten minutes — even when a howling headwind snatched the calls and whistles from my mouth and flung them over my shoulder. She couldn't possibly have heard me. But she always came. Even when I showed up unexpectedly in the afternoon to take her for a family swim in the lake, she came. At these times, I asked Chris and Jill if she'd just been hanging around in the cove all day. But no, they said, they hadn't seen her at all.

I began to wonder if Cecily had another sense that alerted her when I arrived, if seals had some sort of telepathy.

Of course, showing up did not necessarily mean getting out of the water. Like a child involved in a fun outdoor game and ignoring her parents calls to come in for dinner, sometimes it took Cecily fifteen to twenty minutes to obey my increasingly impatient cries — "Cecily come in, NOW!" She'd paddle about in the cove, popping up now and then to make sure I was still there.

As annoying as this could be, I understood. It was hard for Cecily to leave the element in which she felt so free and full of grace. And there was so much to explore out there. At home, limited by walls and her own hunching gait, it must have felt increasingly like living in a cage. She was down to just four bottles a day — one in the morning, one before I dropped her off at the Humphreys', one in the evening, and another late at night. I wondered if she was teaching herself how to catch fish.

In the evenings, when I brought Cecily home, she continued to be possessive of me — much more so than in the water. She knew she was clumsy in this dry element, and had no fast and sure escape from danger as she did in the sea. She depended on me to protect her, and stayed close until I put her down for a nap in the spare room after her dinner bottle.

At about 11:30 every night, when the rest of the family was in bed, she'd call me from the spare room with her whooping, demanding her last bottle. I'd bring her into the living room, and with her curled up on my crossed legs, a quilt wrapped around both of us, I'd feed her while watching *The Tonight Show with Johnny Carson* on TV. When she finished her bottle, she stayed curled up in our quilt tent until the end of the show. I'm not sure what she got out of Johnny's patter, but I know she enjoyed the company. I did, too.

It seemed to be the perfect arrangement — the perfect compromise between a creature of the sea and a creature of the land. Why couldn't we just go on like this indefinitely? I wondered.

The thing is, I wasn't alone in this venture. I was not going to be the one to decide how long Cecily and I would share our two worlds. Steve Katona and the wildlife warden had not granted us permission to rescue the pup so that the Lincolns could add a new member to the family, or so that I would have a companion for late-night TV watching. From the start, it had been made clear that our goal was to get the pup healthy and fat, and then attempt to reintroduce her back to the wild seal colony from which she had almost certainly come.

This colony is about three miles north of Pretty Marsh Harbor, right where at low tide a collection of rocky ledges juts out of the Trenton Narrows, a mile-wide gut formed by the western edge of MDI and the mainland. Dozens and dozens of harbor seal females gather at this "rookery" each spring to whelp their pups, wean them, and then welcome the bull seals back for mating season.

When the water covers the ledges, the females take their pups into the sea and let them nurse while riding on their bellies. Seen from the shore of Mount Desert Island, the ledges look like any other outcrop at low tide. But a pair of binoculars will reveal that almost all the exposed granite surfaces of these reefs are covered in seal — adult seals, weighing up to 250 pounds, lying back to back, side to side, or on their bellies with their heads and tails up, looking like giant furry bananas. And this is just one of the colonies that in the summer populate the waters off MDI.

At an estimated 15,000, this area has one of the largest populations of harbor seals along the Atlantic Coast. This is an astonishing comeback from the late nineteenth century, when a bounty was placed on harbor seals. The idea was to drastically

reduce the population because fishermen believed that seals depleted the fish harvest. Only after several Maine colonies had been almost wiped out, with no significant increase to the fish catches, did the state remove the bounty in 1905. There are, however, still a few fishermen who believe that seals are significant rivals, and even, despite evidence to the contrary, that they enjoy a good lobster as much as any lobster pound patron. Although it is now illegal to kill harbor seals, from time to time a body does wash ashore, the apparent victim of foul play. But the greatest danger seals face from humans — except where they are still legally hunted by aboriginal people — is pollution, propellers, and entanglement in fishing gear.

I often tried to imagine what had happened on that rookery the day Cecily was born. How had she gotten separated from her mother? In my subsequent reading about seals, and in conversations with Steve, I had learned that it really is a rare thing for a mother seal to abandon a healthy baby. Even when their pups are stillborn, some females will stay with the little corpse for days, even weeks, trying to revive it. Steve told me about the time a crew from COA had intervened to remove a dead pup because its mother was starving herself to death, refusing to leave the rookery and her unresponsive baby to fish for herself.

But if some perceived danger startles the females of the rookery when they are whelping — and therefore without bulls to protect them — mass pandemonium can occur, with the new mothers scrambling to get into the water and safety, sometimes forgetting, or even crushing, their babies in their panic. One of the biggest causes of this sort of mass panic is kayakers. While sailboats, and even big noisy motor boats, can pass relatively close to a rookery without so much as disturbing a whisker, a flotilla of kayaks — or even a single one — can instigate one of these terrible stampedes. Something about the needle-like shape of the kayak and its upright paddler must prompt this flight response. It might be an inbred instinct, sparked by the kayaks' resemblance to sharks, a significant seal predator, or perhaps it's a more learned response, passed down from a time when seals were hunted from low-slung canoes and, yes, kayaks.

In recent years, kayaking had become more prevalent in this area, with several excursion companies operating out of Bar Harbor. Steve said that he had already spoken with the owners of these companies and asked them to steer clear of the rookeries until the pups were safely weaned, and they had been receptive. Still, all it took was one lone paddler who just had to come in for a closer look. I could picture newborn Cecily tumbling off the ledge as her mother, perhaps an inexperienced one, fled in panic. Then I imagined her drifting with the tide down the narrows and into our little Pretty Marsh Harbor, where finally, cold, exhausted, and hungry, she clambered out onto my uncle's shore, finding a cold rock for comfort.

Now, as a foster seal mother, I was, as closely as humanly possible, trying to match my behavior toward Cecily with that of the colony females. Already, the seal mothers were leaving their babies for longer stretches of time, which is why I was doing the same with Cecily.

We knew what was going on in the colony because we had a spy. A Smithsonian-based researcher named Susan Wilson had come to Mount Desert Island to study seals that spring under the auspices of Allied Whale. For the purposes of her own research, Susan had stationed herself in a blind on a narrow lump of an island topped off with a scraggly stand of spruce trees, a couple of hundred yards from the rookery

where the wild pups were being raised. The blind, which I got to see once, consisted of a lean-to made from branches covered with a dark green canvas tarpaulin — the sort of shelter I remember having to construct during my Girl Scout camping days. All it contained was a single fold-up chair and some metal boxes for keeping paper and food dry. Since seals are only observable at low tide, when they gather on or around the exposed ledges, Susan would row out to the blind on the outgoing tide and leave when the tide covered the ledges and the colony dispersed. She spent roughly eight hours a day, in all but the worst weather, at her post, keeping track of the wild seals' activities with the help of a powerful set of binoculars, a telescope, and a camera. Coincidentally, Susan's research and Allied Whale's pup rescue program dovetailed, and Susan had agreed to report back to Steve any information she thought might be pertinent to raising and weaning an orphaned pup.

Eventually, the MDI shorefront that faced the colony would be the place from which Cecily would reenter her life as a wild seal. Steve had already received permission from the landowners to use their property as a release site.

We would not take Cecily to this area until that day arrived. If she got used to coming out of the water here to find her mom and a warm bottle waiting, we worried it might interfere with her integrating into the wild colony when the time came. We hoped that by keeping the place strange to her, her natural instincts would kick in and warn her away from the shore.

Susan's island blind was located about halfway between this shore and the rookery. Because she spent most of her days there, I only got to meet with her a few times, but she was a definite presence in my life with Cecily.

The first time Susan and I did meet did not go all that well. When she arrived one morning at the log house to take Cecily's weight and measurements, discuss her food intake, and observe her activity level, the object of her interest had gone missing.

The kids and I simply couldn't find Cecily. She wasn't in the spare room, the doghouse, under the kitchen table, or any of the other usual Cecily hang-outs. Susan stood by, her brow creased, clipboard in hand, as we all raced about the house calling "Cecilee!"

"I found her!" Benjamin finally yelled from upstairs. "Someone forgot to put the gate up!"

I distinctly remembered closing the gate a good half hour before, after Bob had left for work, and when I thought Cecily was napping in the spare room. But she must have made her daring voyage up the stairs before that, while I was still talking to Bob. I had simply closed the gate after her.

Ben had found Cecily sleeping under Bob's and my bed, with Nahvoo quietly keeping guard at the bed's foot.

When we all emerged from the house, laughing about Cecily's big adventure in the land of Upstairs, Susan just stared at us like an owl and jotted something down in her notebook. "Lost the seal," I imagined her writing, or "Forgot to put up safety gate — irresponsible behavior." Even when Cecily proceeded to put on one of her best adorable-seal-pup routines — belly rolls in the grass, peeking her head through my legs, and generally whooping it up — Susan didn't crack a smile.

Of course, Susan, quite rightly, was taking an objective, scientific approach to the whole endeavor. She was always extremely careful that nothing she did out at the blind interfered with or altered the natural behavior of her subjects. By her lights, a seal gamboling on the front lawn of a house, playing peek-a-boo, climbing stairs, and hiding under a bed must have seemed wrong, wrong, wrong, and not at all cute.

I, on the other hand, had lost all semblance of objectivity the moment Cecily was placed in my arms, and couldn't imagine anyone not being charmed by her antics.

But Susan's knowledge of wild seal behavior, based on her observations of this MDI rookery and her past research work, would be the most crucial element in Cecily's successful return to her colony, not my devotion.

Anyway, after that disastrous beginning, we did get Cecily weighed (twenty-five pounds), measured (almost three feet), and I was able to tell Susan exactly how much she was eating and how often, because I had written it all out in a journal Steve had asked me to keep. When I pulled this notebook out of my jacket pocket to show Susan, I wished I hadn't decorated the cover with a collage of colored paper and a cut-out photo of Cecily in the center. It didn't look at all scientific; it looked like the baby books I was keeping for Ben and Alexandra.

After this, I was always a bit intimidated by Susan, and it got in the way of forming any kind of friendship. But even if everything had gone perfectly that first meeting, and she'd been as fun as a car full of circus clowns, I probably would not have taken a shine to Susan. She was eventually going to be the one to tell me when my days as a seal mom were over.

One of these days, the wild mother seals would quite suddenly disappear from the rookery, leaving their babies to whoop and cry and swim about in a frantic search for them. You'd think nature could have worked out something a little kinder, but this is how seals wean their pups. When the mothers return after a week or so, the pups are on their own.

When Susan saw the mother seals vanish, she would be the one to alert Steve that it was time for me to vanish, also, and just as suddenly, from Cecily's life. This was not someone I was destined to like.

Chapter Seven

Someone I did like, immensely, was the other seal mom of Mount Desert Island, a woman from Bass Harbor named Ellen Dupuy. Ellen was my best friend, and the mother of Ben's best friend, Max — who did, incidentally, get to play with the "all work, no play" boy again.

When I called Ellen to tell her about how we had found Cecily and were being allowed to raise her, I explained the program at COA for fostering abandoned pups. There had been a high incidence of abandonment that spring, largely due to an outbreak of seal distemper. After we talked, Ellen had immediately called COA to volunteer her services if they needed someone to raise another pup. Two days later, Lucille arrived.

Ellen also had a difficult time at first getting Lucille to nurse from a bottle. But I had told her about my success with a sponge, and Ellen's teenage daughter Niki finally got Lucille to suck from a nipple with a sponge wrapped around it. Perhaps if I had tried that first, it would have worked with Cecily, too, and we wouldn't have had to go through that messy sponge-wedge stage.

Ellen's situation was far better suited to raising a seal pup than mine. She lived near the head of Bass Harbor, just a minute's walk down to the water from her house. So Lucille, who was probably a few days older than Cecily, and about five pounds heavier, was introduced to the ocean only a day after she arrived. Lucille had never had time to forget that she belonged in the water. After an initial reluctance to leave Ellen and her daughter, both of whom she seemed to regard as her mothers, Lucille was soon swimming about on her own. What's more, when she was hungry, she'd just hunch up the path to the house and call for her bottle. At night, Lucille slept under Ellen and her husband Bill's bed.

Ellen and I talked by phone almost daily. We were like two parents of children with a rare condition, able to share some of the problems and worries that concerned us, as well as the successes and fun stuff.

I told Ellen about teaching Cecily how to swim in the lake, and the crazy lady of Pretty Marsh Harbor story. She told me about the time the adventurous Lucille had disappeared from the harbor and eventually showed up at, of all places, Seal Harbor beach, a good five miles down the coast. This impromptu appearance delighted a busload of tourists, who must have felt they had gotten their money's worth that day. Ellen had been notified by Park Rangers, who had been put on alert by Allied Whale to look out for two seal pups behaving strangely around humans. When she drove over to Seal Harbor, Ellen found a group of people on the beach crowded around and gawking at Lucille, who had suddenly appeared in their midst and started barking at them. Ellen walked through the crowd, picked Lucille up, explaining, "Sorry, she's my seal," then carried her back to the car and drove off.

On another afternoon, after Ellen had left Lucille in the harbor and gone off to some event or other, her housekeeper had seen Lucille come hunching up the path toward the house — apparently tired of swimming for the day and ready for her bottle. In a panic, the housekeeper called the only number she saw by the phone. It turned out to belong to an eminent professor in Canada with whom Ellen's husband Bill had been corresponding on some business matter. "The seal is out of the water," the woman breathlessly informed the baffled professor. Later that night, when Bill talked to him, the professor said that he thought he'd mistakenly received a message in spy code, something having to do with nefarious Russian submarine maneuvers.

As much as we enjoyed talking on the phone, Ellen's and my busy schedules with kids and seal pups had prevented us from getting together. But another important lesson Cecily and Lucille needed to learn before they entered the seal colony was how to socialize with other pups.

So about a three weeks into our foster care, Ellen and I arranged a play date with Ben and Max, Cecily and Lucille.

After leaving Alexandra off at her own play group, Ben and I drove with Cecily over to Bass Harbor. When I unloaded Cecily out of the car, Ellen came out of her house to meet us, with Lucille, of course, flip-flopping after her. If I hadn't known better, I might have thought Lucille was a whole different species of seal. While Cecily was dark and dappled, Lucille was a pale uniform silver on her back, head, and sides, and almost pure white on her belly. But then, a seal might

have thought Ellen and I were different species. While we were roughly the same size and shape, I had shoulder-length blond hair, blue eyes, and an overbite, and Ellen had short dark auburn hair, green eyes, and a dazzling big smile. When Cecily and Lucille met nose-to-nose on Ellen's lawn, a great sneezing and slapping fest ensued, after which both pups turned tail to hide behind their respective mother's legs.

"Why don't we take them down to the water?" Ellen suggested. "Maybe they'll feel more comfortable with each other there."

Ben and Max, who already felt very comfortable with each other, opted to stay up at the house to work on some refinements in their space program. Ellen's daughter Niki, Lucille's other mother, was off somewhere being a teenager.

Ellen and I and the two pups headed down the dirt path toward the shore. It was quite a ways, and I noticed how much better, or at least faster, Lucille was at land travel than Cecily. Lucille had been making this trip every day for three weeks or so, and presumably had just gotten good at it, while my spoiled Cecily was enjoying limousine service, and more recently, wheelbarrow rides.

I was a little concerned about letting Cecily swim in this harbor. Bass Harbor is a big commercial fishing community, vying with Southwest Harbor as the Island's largest. At the end of the nineteenth century, and for sixty years after, a big Underwood sardine-packing plant operated here, employing most of the adults in the village. When the men in their herring boats arrived every day save Sunday, filled to the gunwales with fish they had caught in their seines, a steam whistle was sounded, and the women would walk to the factory to cut and pack the sardines into those traditional square tin cans with the key attached. I had met women who'd worked their entire adult lives on this packing line, their hands still scarred from the hundreds of nicks they inflicted on themselves in the process. And yet every one of them spoke about working shoulder-to-shoulder with their women friends and neighbors as good times, and expressed regret that in the fifties the plant had finally closed after the herring harvest had been depleted by decades of overfishing.

After years of trying to preserve the handsome brick building that once housed all this activity as a maritime-related facility, the town finally succumbed to development pressures. It is now being renovated into luxury shorefront condominiums.

The sardine plant is gone, but Bass Harbor is still one of the most active fishing villages on the Island, with dozens of lobster boats and scallop draggers moored in the harbor, and several large wharves to receive their catch when they come in from a day's fishing. And every weekday morning, when they rev up their diesel engines, it sounds like a stock car rally.

Although the head of the harbor, where Ellen and Bill lived, is shallow and relatively free of all this boat traffic, I worried that Cecily might follow the wayward Lucille out into the main harbor, and not being as savvy about boats as Lucille, get hurt. It was kind of like letting an older city kid take my country kid for a trip into town.

But as it turned out, neither pup was particularly interested in going any great distance, and both were content to paddle about in the shallow water. Ellen and I, wearing our bathing suits, waded out to our thighs in the cold water, which only became tolerable after our legs went numb. Each of the two pups spent most of their swim time circling her respective mom, only occasionally wandering out a short distance before resuming the circling. This was different from their normal, more adventurous, behavior, and Ellen and I suspected that although they pretended to be oblivious of each other, they were both very aware that a strange and possibly untrustworthy creature had entered the picture.

In the water, Cecily and Lucille looked almost identical, but Ellen and I had no trouble telling them apart. Their cries were different, for one thing — Lucille had more of a bark than a whoop. They behaved differently in the water, too. Cecily was a performer, executing her belly rolls and other underwater tricks, like swimming between my legs and through a hoop made of my arms. Lucille swam from here to there and back again without making a big show of it. Cecily, of course, was comfortable swimming and playing with people. Lucille, however, did almost all of her swimming alone. Her foster mom had grown up in Florida, where they jump into heated pools from a diving board, not into the North Atlantic from the deck of a sailboat. Waist-deep was as far as Ellen went.

After about ten minutes of successfully avoiding one another, Cecily and Lucille accidentally decided to explore the base of the same rock. The water was shallow enough for Ellen and me to clearly see them underwater as they each approached the rock from opposite sides. When they both came around the corner and met face-to-face, they shot to the surface, coming halfway out of the water in a plume of spray. They batted at each other as they came, then peeled off in opposite directions. After we stopped laughing, Ellen remarked, "Gosh, I sure hope they're better behaved with the wild pups out there."

It made us both think about the time we would have to give up our foster daughters. Once again, it was good to have someone with whom to share my very mixed feelings about that looming event.

We did make another play date for the two pups, though, this time in Cecily's territory, Long Pond. Not at Pond's End, which was too crowded now for even one seal, but a more secluded spot Bob and I had discovered at the far end of one of the park roads in Pretty Marsh.

After hearing about the Lincoln family swims with Cecily, Lucille's family wanted to experience what it was like. That weekend, both families met with our seals at the lake for a picnic. We had the place all to ourselves, and except for the occasional passing motorboat in the distance towing a water skier, our outing was undisturbed.

Lucille and Cecily got along much better here. They didn't actually play together, but they didn't get into a flipper fight if they happened to run into each other either. Lucille was at first a little flummoxed to find her whole family – plus a

bunch of strangers — in the water with her, and steered clear of all the splashing and screeching of the kids. But eventually, her curiosity overcame her shyness and she got downright playful. Cecily as ever was a clown.

When we weren't in the water, Ellen and I sat on the shore and talked as we fed our pups their bottles, just like a couple of moms with new babies to care for, while the older kids and their dads cavorted in the lake. And just like new mothers, we competitively compared our babies' various talents and cleverness, increasingly exaggerating to the point where we were claiming Cecily and Lucille could recite the alphabet and do simple addition.

We also talked a little more seriously about what it was going to be like to have to give up our talented, clever pups. But at that point, it still seemed like a long way off, and we didn't dwell on it.

This was Lucille's one and only freshwater outing, and as it turned out, one of the last for Cecily. As she became increasingly at home in the cove, I could no longer justify picking her up to take her for family swims in the lake. By late June, Cecily's days as a freshwater seal were over. Soon my days of swimming with Cecily ended as well.

Three weeks after that day with Lucille at Long Pond, Steve called to say that it was time to start seriously preparing Cecily for the day she would return to the wild. It didn't seem like much time had passed at all.

It was the first week of July, and Susan had reported that the wild seal mothers were beginning to wean their pups. We only had a about two weeks to get Cecily ready for her release date.

Part of the preparation was to start eliminating the unseal-like events in her day. It was time, Steve said, to leave Cecily out at sea all night.

As much as I wanted to protest, I knew he was probably right. Cecily had fattened up so nicely she was positively roly-poly. She was also becoming increasingly confident at sea, taking longer and longer to come in when I called her. And even when she did come in, she didn't always seem all that interested in her bottle, which suggested that she was finding something far more exciting to eat than creamed, mashed smelts. But she always seemed happy to see me, and willing to clamber into the wheelbarrow for the ride up to the car.

That day, while Cecily was at sea, I spent a few hours in the garden, where the weeds and slugs were now battling me for possession of all the tender green shoots and fronds that had appeared in the crooked ranks I'd planted.

I kept seeing Cecily's empty doghouse by the corner of the house and half-wishing she was in it, having a snooze before coming down to join me. Then I had what I thought was good idea and called Steve.

"What if we left the doghouse out on the shore for Cecily tomorrow night?" I asked. "She thinks of it as a shelter, and if she gets lonely or frightened she can just wait for me in there 'til morning. At least until she gets used to being out at night."

"No, Nan," Steve said. "You really have to help her learn that the shore isn't a safe shelter for her. I know it's hard for you to accept this now, but her safety is at sea."

I thought about Cecily coming ashore at night at some distant place and deciding to take shelter in a shorefront boathouse, or, God forbid, a real doghouse with a real dog in it — a mean dog. I saw Steve's point, and Cecily's house stayed where it was.

The following day, after her morning bottle, the kids and I drove with Cecily, as usual, down to the Humphreys'. Although it was a lovely warm day, this time we didn't join Cecily for a swim. As Susan and Steve had advised, swimming with humans was something it would be better for her to forget. Perhaps, but I knew I would never forget it.

After a while, when Cecily realized I wouldn't be joining her, she took off like a kid with more important things to do than hang out with boring mom. I wondered if she was meeting other seals out there, making friends. Or was she, as in her first encounter with Lucille, slapping and snorting at them and refusing to recognize these other aquatic creatures as kin?

At about five o'clock that evening I returned and started calling her in. She appeared quickly, after ten minutes or so, and even agreed to come ashore after a few further calls. But this time, when she clambered out onto the beach, I didn't have the wheelbarrow waiting to take her back to the VW. Instead, I skootched down beside her and offered her a bottle, which she accepted.

When she'd finished, I waded into the water. "Come on Cecily," I called. "This is your home now."

She hesitated, confused, I guess, at this change in routine. But eventually she splashed out to me, and before long her little black head was bobbing out of the cove.

It would still be light out for several hours and I had asked Chris Humphrey to please come down and check for Cecily a couple of times before it got dark — not to call her, but just to make sure she didn't decide to come home on her own. Chris's mom, Jill, said she would check a final time before she went to bed and would listen for any whooping coming from the harbor. She said she'd call me at home if she heard or saw anything to concern her.

There was nothing more I could do but worry, so I did a lot of that.

I awoke early the next morning after a restless night, half the time expecting the phone to ring and half the time hoping it wouldn't, and trying to figure out which would make me happier, silence, or Jill calling to say Cecily was crying out in the harbor and to come quick. Jill didn't call, however, and I never did come up with an answer to that question.

I threw on my clothes and drove down to the Humphreys'. From the farmhouse I could see Chris's blond head down on the shore, facing the water. I ran to join her. She pointed out into the cove, and following her finger I could see Cecily traversing back and forth between the two shores like a tacking sailboat.

"I didn't call her," Chris said, "But I think she wants to come in, she's been doing that for about a half hour.

On one hand, I was pleased that Cecily hadn't come in on her own, without being called; on the other hand, I felt terrible that after having left her to spend a whole night all by herself out in that cold and lonely ocean, I hadn't at least been there to greet her in the morning.

I had to remind myself that my not being there to greet her was something she needed to get used to.

But now I called her. "Cecilee!" She stopped, stretched her head toward my voice, saw me, and rather lazily zigzagged her way to shore. In addition to her usual bottle, I had brought along a bag full of whole smelts. Although it seemed pretty obvious that Cecily was finding food for herself at sea, I had never actually seen her eat a whole fish, and this worried me. I had tried several times to get her interested in the unblended smelts or herring I bought at A.V. Higgins, and she always, literally, turned her nose up at them. I tried again now, but she lunged for the bottle instead. I hid the bottle and offered the fish. No go.

"Okay, no more fooling around, Cecily," I said sternly.

"You are going to eat this damn fish." This time I grabbed her muzzle, and while she fought me, pried her mouth open and jammed the fish in. *Ackk! Ackk!* she protested, but the fish slipped down her throat. Seals don't chew their food. The second one went down a little easier, then a third.

"Good girl," I said, stroking her head. "If you don't know it already, you're just going to love these things, especially when they're all warm and wriggly and running away." Then I offered her the bottle, which she chugalugged, as if to say, "Yeah, maybe, but this stuff is still the best."

After she was fed, Chris and I played with her in the water for a few minutes, letting her dive between our legs and slip away when we tried to catch her in our arms. And then she was gone. When we saw her next, she was halfway out of the harbor. I have to say I felt a little pang of jealousy. What was so compelling out there that it could draw her away from me and the little time we had to spend together? Years later, I would be reminded of this feeling when Ben and Alexandra started making their own plans without including mom and dad.

Chapter Eight

One afternoon, Susan called and asked if Ellen and I would like to take a trip down to Rockport to meet Harry Goodridge, Andre's dad. I certainly did, and Ellen, who was also leaving Lucille out at night, agreed it would be a good way to spend an evening without constantly worrying about our pups.

We two seal moms were slightly hysterical that night as we drove to Rockland. Our nervousness about our pups translated into some serious silliness and teasing of the ever-serious Susan. She was on a fact-finding mission, while we were just eager to talk with a seal dad.

"So, who gets Harry?" Ellen asked. "Do we arm wrestle, flip a coin or what?"

"Oh, I think we should see who can hold their breath the longest," I replied. After which the two of us held a breath-holding competition, punctuated by cries of "I know you're cheating, you're sipping breaths! Come on, Susan, you try! You could use a seal-man in your life." Then we launched into a chorus of Sam and Dave's "He's a Soul Man" — only, of course, in our version it was "He's a Seal Man," with other appropriate lyric changes. We laughed so hard we could hardly breathe and were in grave danger of wetting our pants in the back seat of Susan's car.

Susan was not amused. Forced to endure one-and-a-half hours of our foolishness, she occasionally threatened to put us out of the car if we didn't stop behaving like five-year-olds. She was absolutely right that we were behaving like children, and it was a welcome relief from the reality of being worried mothers.

By the time we reached Harry's, we had sobered up some and were able to carry on a reasonably intelligent conversation, just so long as Ellen and I didn't make eye contact. I made the mistake once, and Ellen mouthed the words "Seal Man" at me. I had to cover the guffaw welling up in my throat with a coughing fit. Harry got me a glass of water, while Ellen sat there with her legs primly crossed at the ankles, looking as composed as the hostess of a Junior League tea party.

Harry was a nice guy. He was in his sixties now, and it was about his fifteenth year as Andre's dad. Andre had been set loose at Marblehead just a week before, and Harry was still waiting for his return to Rockport. When Andre did arrive, Harry and he had a little act they would perform for the tourists, until winter, when it was time for Andre to return to the aquarium.

It was interesting to learn how, after plucking the inquisitive little seal out of the water some fifteen years ago, Harry had managed to get Andre to feed. He had encountered the same problems we had getting the pup to nurse from a bottle, but eventually, he'd carved a groove in a wooden barrel, covered it in neoprene — a rubbery substance — drilled a hole through it all, and then stuck in a bottle nipple. Definitely a guy's way of nurturing. It never would have occurred to me. Once fed, Andre had become imprinted on Harry and was, it seemed, happy to learn a few tricks to wow the crowds who gathered in Rockport harbor to see Harry and his famous seal perform. If Mr. Goodridge had started out this venture as a lark, or as a possible money-making scheme, there was no doubt how much he cared for Andre now. Every spring for the past ten years, ever since Andre started wintering at the aquarium, he anxiously awaited Andre's return, concerned about the boats, fishing gear, sharks, and other dangers he might find on his way home. In this, Ellen and I had definite common ground with Harry Goodridge.

We also envied him to some degree. While Andre had never become a member of a wild seal colony, and it was unlikely he had been able to win a mate, he and Harry *had* been able to form a lifelong relationship. We would only have this one summer.

Our trip home was a lot quieter and more reflective.

Meanwhile, I'd been going down to the Humphreys' every morning and every evening with a bottle and a bag of fish since I'd begun to leave Cecily out at night. Although sometimes I now had to wait up to a half hour for her to appear, she always showed up.

And then, one rainy morning, she didn't. After calling for a good hour or so, I finally gave up and drove home, shivering with cold and concern. The Humphreys weren't home, so I couldn't ask them to keep watch for her. I went back over there several times that day and called while the kids waited in the car.

"Is she lost?" Ben asked after our second trip.

"Oh no, sweetie," I said with more assurance than I felt. "I'm sure she's just having a good time and doesn't feel like coming home right now. Maybe she's playing with friends. When she's hungry she'll come — just like you come in when you want something to eat."

I was right. Cecily did come in that evening. I had brought two bottles, in case she was ravenous, but she only accepted one before flopping back into the water.

In the following few days, Cecily continued to establish her own routine. Sometimes she showed, sometimes she didn't. Of course, I worried when she didn't appear, thinking about those boat propellers, sea monsters, and what have you. But, gradually, less and less. I began to believe she was finding her own way out there, learning to be a wild seal all by herself.

So who needed Steve and Susan to tell me when and where I should end this relationship?

It seemed perfectly reasonable to let things go on as they were. I'd spend the next twenty-five years or so making occasional visits to the shore, and Cecily, when she had the time and inclination, would come and meet me — like a married daughter who has a life and home of her own, but occasionally needs a little motherly loving. What could be wrong with that?

Actually, there was plenty wrong with that.

For one thing, if Cecily didn't become integrated with a wild colony, she probably wouldn't migrate south with them to Cape Cod, Massachusetts, or Long Island, New York, when the harbor began icing up in the winter. An iced-up harbor is no place for a seal to be. They can get trapped under the ice and drown, or be crushed by the shifting sheets as they break up and grind against each other. As a lone seal, Cecily might, like Andre, not find a mate, have pups of her own, and live out her seal destiny. What if she became a nuisance in the harbor, swamping boats, stealing bait? While fishermen no longer shoot seals over fishing rights, a particularly annoying seal might ignite that old animosity.

My life could change, too. What if I couldn't always be there for her?

All very good reasons for doing everything I could to make sure Cecily lived the rest of her life as a totally — not half-wild — seal.

But when I got the call from Steve, telling me that the mother seals were leaving the rookery, none of those reasons seemed to matter. I listened numbly as he said that I was to call Cecily in the next morning and bring her over to the release site. But first, I could feed her one last time.

After I hung up the phone, I called Ellen. Susan had called her with the news, too. But something else had changed.

Judging from where she had been found, Steve believed that Lucille had probably come from a different colony than Cecily — another large seal community near Swan's Island, about five miles off Bass Harbor. Ellen had been told that when the time came, they would be releasing Lucille in that vicinity. However, Steve and Susan were now having second thoughts. Since Susan could only observe from one place, and because she had no counterpart near the Swan's Island colony, they had decided to release the two pups together. This news made Ellen and me feel a little better. Even though the pups hadn't exactly become pals at their two encounters, they did at least know each other. And perhaps with no mothers to turn to, they would turn to each other.

I told Bob and the kids what was happening. Although Ben and Alexandra had seen very little of Cecily since she'd been spending so much time at sea, and had gone back to their other interests — spaceships, toys and playmates — they were both sad knowing they would probably never see her again.

"Why can't we just go visit her sometime?" Benjamin asked.

"Because she needs to be part of her seal family now, not ours," I explained. "But we will always remember her and love her, and maybe she will remember us a little, too — but not enough to make her sad."

As I said all this, in the back of my mind I was working out other scenarios. Cecily wouldn't show up at the Humphreys' for days, or weeks, maybe, and then, well, it would probably be too late for her to join the wild colony, and she'd just have to be the resident seal of Pretty Marsh Harbor. Or perhaps, after she was dropped off, she'd be like Andre and keep returning to her home harbor, demonstrating her choice to maintain a relationship with her human family.

I wasn't thinking clearly. If any of these things happened, it would only demonstrate that I had failed in my most important duty as Cecily's foster mother — to let her go. I just didn't think I could bear to say good-bye.

But I did.

The next morning, Cecily showed up within a half hour of my calling and, I think, seemed rather surprised to find the wheelbarrow back in the picture. Still, after drinking half the bottle I brought her and refusing the smelts — preferring the wriggly ones she was catching on her own, I hoped, she allowed Bob and me to load her up and trundle her up through the hay field for the last time, to the VW van where Ben and Alexandra were waiting with the Humphreys. As we drove away, Jenny and Chris waved mournfully after us. It had been a while since Cecily had been in a car, but she remembered her favorite position whenever I was in the passenger seat, and she draped herself across my feet.

The area we were going to was called Indian Point — one of the traditional landing places for Native Americans when they set out from Trenton, just a mile or so across Western Bay from the MDI shore. The property at the end of a long wooded dirt road was another saltwater farm — smaller than the Humphreys', and with an antique apple orchard rather than a hayfield sloping toward its bowl-shaped cove.

Susan, Steve, Ellen, and her family were all waiting when we arrived. Steve was carrying a can of yellow paint, and Susan a can of red paint. While we settled Cecily and Lucille on the ground, Steven proceeded to paint a wide yellow stripe down Cecily's back, and Susan painted a red stripe on Lucille. Both pups snorted and scooted away. But the deed was accomplished.

Another notice had been put in the *Bar Harbor Times*, requesting that if anyone saw a small seal with a yellow stripe

or a red stripe down its back to call either Steve Katona at COA, the Wildlife Department, the Acadia National Park rangers, Ellen, or me. If either of the two seals separated herself from the wild colony, this could be a way of tracking her.

It wasn't until I saw that horrible yellow stripe on Cecily's back that I really believed what was about to happen. I looked over at Ellen, and her stricken face said the reality had just hit her, too. This time we had to avoid eye contact to keep from crying.

When the paint had dried, Susan said it was time. But she said it kindly, recognizing that this was going to be a difficult moment for the two families.

In something like a trance, I walked down through the orchard, onto the beach and to the water's edge. Bob followed with Ben and Alexandra. Ellen's family picked a spot several yards away to have their own private last moments with Lucille.

I could see Ben was close to tears, but there was no way he was going to cry with Max, who was almost a year younger, in the vicinity. Alexandra was whimpering softly, and I really think she understood that we were saying good-by to our little seal, although I'm sure she didn't know why. At this point, I wasn't sure myself. Bob took the kids' hands, and we all waded into the water. Of course, Cecily followed. She swam around us for a little while, allowing me to stroke her sleek sides and head, which left a few streaks of yellow on my palms, and then, bored with my melancholy play and curious, I'm sure, about this new place I had brought her to, swam away. I watched her shiny black head as she swam out toward the wild seal colony. I could hear the distant whoops and barks of the other seal pups calling for their mothers. Then there was another dark little head bobbing along behind her — Lucille. About fifty yards out, Cecily's head popped beneath the surface, and without a ripple, she disappeared into her new life as a wild seal. After swimming along for a few more strokes, Lucille followed.

There wasn't much to say and do after that. Ellen and I knew exactly how the other was feeling, so we just said good-bye to Steve and Susan, walked back to our cars, and drove home. On the drive, Cecily's half-full baby bottle rolled back and forth between the seats.

Over the following two days, Susan and Steve gave Ellen and me regular reports on our pups. Both had stayed in the general area of the rookery and had been spotted swimming with the other pups. We were elated. It seemed that everything was going to work out just as we had all hoped.

But on day three, Susan called Steve to report that Cecily had gone missing from the colony. Steve called me with the news but said not to worry; after three days, she would be familiar enough with the area to find her way back to the colony when she wanted to.

So I tried not to worry until the following day, when another call came. This time Steve said he had heard from a family who lived along the banks of the Pretty Marsh salt marsh. They had apparently been barbecuing on their lawn when a seal pup with a yellow stripe down its back suddenly clambered out of the marsh and hunched its way toward them. It whooped a few times, and they threw it a couple of sardines, which the pup ignored. Then it returned to the water and swam away.

Again, Steve told me not to worry.

I wasn't worried, I was frantic. I was certain Cecily was trying to find her way home to the harbor, but had gotten lost in the marsh. It was one of those alternative scenarios I had played out in my head these past few days. In my imagination she had always found her way safely home. But now she was out there, lost and alone. Maybe hungry, too, just as she had been when she was separated from her real mom. So I hustled the kids into the car and drove along Indian Point Road, dipping down into every driveway that might reach the shore. Most of these drives ended in some very fancy summer homes, where caretakers were busy preparing the estates for the imminent return of their owners.

"Um, I'm just looking for my seal," I explained as I marched the kids past these showcase homes to stand on their private shores and call "Cecilee!" Like the fishermen who had given me such a wide berth in Pretty Marsh Harbor, none of these caretakers challenged me, only stood by as this strange family whistled and shouted, and then drove off. I must have visited at least a dozen of these homes, but no Cecily.

I was frantic, and so I finally called Bob at work, tearfully explaining how Cecily was lost and trying to find her way home.

Bob was concerned, too, and without consulting Steve or Susan, we decided to seriously go look for her. Ellen agreed to bring Max over to the log house to watch Ben and Alexandra for the day. After she arrived, we loaded one of Bob's wooden strip-canoes onto his pickup truck and drove to a causeway that crosses the marsh about midway between its two ocean ends.

It was a strange day. Very warm and absolutely still, with a steamy haze lifting off the water that made the air shimmer. As we paddled down the marsh, I called out "Cecilee!" over and over, surely disturbing the peace of the homeowners along the shore. Nothing. When we reached the ocean, it was as still and flat as a sheet of metal and turned on odd coppery color where the sun reflected off its surface. I continued calling as we paddled down Western Bay heading north toward the wild seal colony. Cecilee, Cecilee!

Brsshh! The head of a seal popped up about five feet from our canoe. Not Cecily, but an enormous piebald bull. It stared at us as we paddled on. I kept calling, my voice echoing between the MDI and Mainland shores — "Cecilee! Cecilee! Cecilee!"

Brsshh! A second seal popped up, this time a fawn-colored female.

By the time we reached Indian Point, I had called up at least eight seals, none of them Cecily. Bob and I were hot and tired now, and decided to beach on one of several small islands — very much like the one Susan had her blind on — to go for a skinny-dip. I remember the water being unusually green when I dove in. The sun slanted through it in beams of a paler green. Below me, big leathery fronds of kelp, outlined in tiny silver air bubbles, waved in the current. On patches of the sea floor were clusters of starfish, forming little constellations in shades of pink interspersed with fuzzy dark brown sand dollars. It was incredibly beautiful, and I kept diving under to see more. Then, just at the edge of my blurred underwater vision, I noticed large dark shapes flitting back and forth about ten feet away. At first I was alarmed — Hey, I'd read *Jaws* — and then I realized they were seals! Six or seven of them darting back and forth as if they were on patrol, checking us out. They never came close enough for me to see clearly, but never moved out of sight either. Vigilant shadows. Bob had seen them, too. When we surfaced together, we were both awestruck and nearly speechless. We dressed and climbed back in the canoe.

"I think we can go home now," I said.

As we paddled back toward Pretty Marsh, I realized that while bathing in the emerald green sea with the beams of light, kelp forest, starfish, and flitting shadows, something important had changed. I was finally going to be able to let Cecily go. I understood now that she had a true community out there — a family of seals keeping watch, making sure that everything was safe and ready to welcome her into their beautiful world when she was finally ready to join them and let me go.

Epilogue

About a month after her release, I received more news of Cecily. A couple with their young son had been picnicking on an island in Bartlett Narrows when a smallish seal emerged from the water and hunched a little way up the shore. When the boy walked toward it offering his sandwich, the seal sneezed — *Tchoo!* — turned about, and flip-flopped back to the water. As they watched it swim away, they noticed it had a few patches of something yellow stuck on its dark, dappled back — pollen, they thought. Cecily was right where she was supposed to be, and as far as I know, it was her last contact with humans.

Ellen and I did get to see Lucille again, though. A week after she had been released with Cecily, Ellen got a call from the Park Rangers saying that a local lobster fisherman from Isle au Haut — another island a few miles off Rockport — had picked up a baby seal that appeared to be wounded. The fisherman had mistaken Lucille's red stripe for blood. Ellen and I both drove down to Rockport to pick Lucille up. She arrived by boat in a lobster crate and seemed delighted to see Ellen again. The same day Lucille was taken back to Indian Point, and released, and then like Cecily was never heard from again.

Ellen and I are still good friends, although she now lives far from seal territory in Santa Fe, New Mexico. When we talk, we often reminisce about our wonderful summer of the seals and get a bit goofy about it all. And at dinner parties and other gatherings, we tend to mix our individual stories together into one long seal story. Susan, I am sure, would not approve.

I still think about Cecily often — well, pretty much always, especially when I'm out in a boat, or walking along the shore. Not too long ago, I was taking just such a walk with a friend on a shore path in Seal Cove, the town next to Pretty Marsh. It was a still, pearly gray day, with a strip of pale gold stretching all along the horizon, separating the flat pewter-colored sea from the sky. We stopped at the end of the point to sit, eat our picnic lunch, and admire the view. A pair of loons cruised by. Then we heard this breathy *whuh! whuh! whuh!* sound coming from behind us, and a few seconds later an osprey came wheeling around the point just feet from where we sat.

It was a magical moment, and as I often do when I'm near the sea on still day such as this, I was inspired to call out "Cecilee!" Almost immediately a dark little head popped up below us in a pool of water between the rocks. It stared at us for a few moments with its big black eyes, then, just as suddenly, disappeared.

It couldn't have been Cecily. After all these years, she would be a *grande dame* of the colony now and much bigger than this young seal. But as we walked back along the shore path,

I remembered how I used to think Cecily had a sixth sense about knowing when I would turn up to call her. Could she have passed this on to her grandchildren?

I like to think so.

— THE END —